Link ◆ Word

ITALIAN
by Association

Dr. Michael M. Gruneberg

Printed on recyclable paper

PASSPORT BOOKS
a division of *NTC Publishing Group*
Lincolnwood, Illinois USA

CONTENTS

759194

SECTION 7

SECTION 8

SECTION 9

SECTION 10

FOREWORD

Anyone reading a book that teaches a foreign language might well wonder why it has been written by a memory expert and not a linguist or a language teacher. Well, the simple fact is that if you want to *remember* what you are taught, then putting ease of remembering at the center of the design of the book is likely to lead to far higher levels of learning than a book written only with the ideas of a linguist in mind. Of course, this book has been written by a memory expert working with skilled linguists so that the language aspects are correct.

The basic "memory idea" of the book to help you remember what you are taught is the "method of association," or the linkword method. Learning a foreign language is all about associating what you are familiar with, e.g., the word *bread,* with something you are not familiar with— the word for *bread* is *pan* in Spanish or Japanese. There are two possible ways you can do this. You can repeat the words *bread* and *pan* together until you are sure it sticks, or you can "picture" yourself putting some bread into a pan. This picturing technique is known as the method of association, or the linkword method. Of course, as far as learning foreign language vocabulary is concerned, there is a further complication that the foreign word may not sound like *any* English word. For example, the Spanish for cow is *vaca,* which sounds like "vaka." What you do in this situation is to imagine a *cow* with a *vacuum* cleaner, cleaning a field. The linkword *vacuum* does not have to be identical to the foreign word in order to be able to associate *cow* with "vaka" through the use of mental pictures. It may sound bizarre, but over fifty studies published in scientific journals have found this technique to materially increase the level of foreign vocabulary learning. In one study of Spanish, for example, learning increased from 28% for rote learning to 88% using the picture association technique.

The method of association was known to the Greeks as an efficient way of improving memory, and the application of the method of association to learning foreign languages was discussed as long ago as the nineteenth century. It is only recently, however, that psychologists have shown how effective the method is when applied to learning foreign language vocabulary, and the present book is, as far as the author is aware, the first to make use of the method to provide a whole course for foreign language learners, teaching not only an extensive vocabulary but providing a basic grammar and using sentence examples.

The course consists of hundreds of useful words that, with the grammar provided, can be strung together to form sentences. In eight to twelve hours, you should be able to go right through the course and acquire enough useful knowledge to communicate when you go abroad.

The author has published a number of studies* of the courses that show how fast and easy people find it. In one study of travel executives, the group was taught Spanish for *twelve* contact hours. They were then tested by an independent test expert who found they were virtually errorless on the four hundred word vocabulary and grammar they had been taught. The independent expert estimated they would normally have taken *forty* hours to reach that standard. In a second study, a group of bankers was taught a vocabulary of at least six hundred words and basic grammar in four days. However, it is not just the linguistically able who benefit from the courses. In one study, thirteen-year-old low-ability language students were given one session every week using the Spanish by Association course and another session using conventional teaching methods for one term. At the end of the term, the students were given a test where the mean vocabulary score on Spanish following conventional teaching was 23.75% compared to 69% for the Spanish by Association course. One student out of sixteen passed with conventional teaching, fourteen out of sixteen passed with Spanish by Association teaching. The studies carried out to date show that the courses are ideal for anyone who wants to learn the basics of a language in a hurry, whether for travel, for business, or for schoolwork. For many people such as the tourist who just wants to get by or the business person who has to be in Berlin next Wednesday, then Paris next Friday, their language needs do not involve the mastery of a single language in depth but the rapid acquisition of a basic language to get by with. Because they are designed specifically to enhance speed and ease of language acquisition and to help

*M. M. Gruneberg and G. C. Jacobs (1991), "In Defence of Linkword," *The Language Learning Journal* (3), 25–29.

you remember what you have learned, the By Association courses are uniquely suited to meet such needs, as well as the needs of those who might have experienced language learning difficulties earlier in life.

INTRODUCTION

WHO IS *ITALIAN BY ASSOCIATION* FOR?

The short answer is that By Association books are for anyone and everyone who wants to learn the basics of a language in a hurry. It can be used by children or by adults. Even young children who cannot read can be taught Italian words by a parent reading out the images.

The By Association courses have been carefully designed to teach you a basic grammar and words in a simple step-by-step way that anyone can follow. After about ten to twelve hours, or even less, you will have a vocabulary of literally hundreds of words and the ability to string these words together to form sentences. The course is ideal, therefore, for the tourist or business person who just wants the basics in a hurry so he or she can be understood, e.g., in the hotel, arriving at the destination, sightseeing, eating out, in emergencies, telling time, and so on.

The course is also an ideal supplement to schoolwork. Many students feel that they remember words for the first time when introduced to the By Association system, and understand basic grammar for the first time too!

HOW TO USE *ITALIAN BY ASSOCIATION*

1. You will be presented with words like this:
   The Italian for **hand** is **mano.**
   Imagine a **man** warming his hand.
   What you do is to imagine this picture in your mind's eye as vividly as possible.

2. After you have read the image for a word, you should visualize it in your mind's eye for about ten seconds before moving on to the next word. If you do not spend enough time thinking about the image, it will not stick in your memory as well as it should.

3. Sometimes the word in Italian and in English is the same or very similar. For example, the word for **taxi** in Italian is **taxi.** When this happens, you will be asked to associate the word in some way with spaghetti.

   Imagine a **taxi** with spaghetti on the seat.

   Whenever spaghetti comes to mind, therefore, you will know the word is the same or similar in English and Italian.

4. The examples given in the course may well strike you as silly and bizarre. They have deliberately been designed in this way to illustrate points of grammar and to get away from the idea that you should remember useful phrases "parrot fashion."

5. **Accents**
   Some Italian words have accents, for example, *sì* (*yes*). However, you should not focus so much on remembering the accents as remembering the words, at least to begin with.

6. Pronunciation

The approximate pronunciation of words is given in parentheses after the word is presented for the first time.

For example: The Italian for **cow** is **mucca** (MOOKKA).
(MOOKKA) is the way the word is pronounced.

Do not worry too much about pronunciation to begin with. The approximate pronunciation given in parentheses will allow you to be understood.

SOME USEFUL HINTS

1. It is usually best to go through the course as quickly as possible. Many people can get through most of the course in a weekend, especially if they start on Friday evening.

2. Take a break of about ten minutes between each section, and always *stop* if you feel tired.

3. Don't worry about forgetting a few words, and do not go back to relearn words you have forgotten. Just think of how much you are learning, and try to pick up the forgotten words when it comes time to review.

4. Review after Section 4, Section 8 and at the end of the course. Then review the whole course a week later and a month later.

5. Don't worry if you forget some of the words or grammar after a time. Relearning is extremely fast, and going through the book for a few hours just before you go abroad will quickly get you back to where you were.

6. The course will not give you conversational fluency. You can't expect this until you go abroad and live in a country for a period of time. What it will give you very rapidly is the ability to survive in a large number of situations you will meet abroad. Once you have gotten this framework, you will find it much easier to pick up more words and grammar when you travel.

IMPORTANT NOTE

The first section of the course can be basically regarded as a training section designed to get you into the By Association method quickly and easily.

After about forty-five minutes, you will have a vocabulary of about thirty words and be able to translate sentences. Once you have finished Section 1, you will have the confidence to go through the rest of the course just as quickly. Animal words are used in the first section as they are a large group of "easy to image" words. Many animal words of course are useful to have as they are often met abroad, e.g., dog, cat, etc., or they are edible!

Finally, when it comes to translating sentences, the answers are given at the bottom of the page. You may find it useful to cover up the answers before you try to do the translations.

SECTION 1

ANIMALS

☐ **Think of each image in your mind's eye for about ten seconds.**
For example, the Italian for **drawer** is **cassetto**. Imagine in your mind's eye for ten seconds putting **cassettes** into a drawer.

　☐ *Note: The word on the right-hand side of the page*
　　(IN PARENTHESES) is the way the word is pronounced.

SOME COMMON ANIMALS

- The Italian for **cat** is **gatto**.　　　　　　　(GATTO)
  Imagine you've **got to** hold a cat.

- The Italian for **bird** is **uccello**.　　　　　(OOCHELLO)
  Imagine telling a bird in an animal orchestra,
  "**You cello,** me conductor."

- The Italian for **goat** is **capra**.　　　　　　(KAPRA)
  Imagine a goat looking up at night at the
  constellation **Capricorn.**

- The Italian for **bull** is **toro**.　　　　　　　(TORO)
  Imagine a **toreador** fighting a bull.

- The Italian for **cow** is **mucca**.　　　　　　(MOOKKA)
  Imagine a cow going moo—a **moo-cow.**

- The Italian for **duck** is **anitra**.　　　　　(ANEETRA)
  Imagine a duck walking along a high wire—
  a neat trick.

- The Italian for **goose** is **oca**.　　　　　　　(OKA)
  Imagine a goose shouting **O.K! O.K!**

- The Italian for **pig** is **porco**.　　　　　　　(PORKO)
  Imagine eating **pork** while riding a pig.

- The Italian for **donkey** is **asino**.　　　　(AZEENO)
  Imagine a donkey looking like an **ass I know.**

- The Italian for **frog** is **rana**.　　　　　　　(RANA)
  Imagine you **ran a** mile after seeing a horrible frog.

7

☐ *You can write your answers in*

- What is the English for **rana**? _____
- What is the English for **asino**? _____
- What is the English for **porco**? _____
- What is the English for **oca**? _____
- What is the English for **anitra**? _____
- What is the English for **mucca**? _____
- What is the English for **toro**? _____
- What is the English for **capra**? _____
- What is the English for **uccello**? _____
- What is the English for **gatto**? _____

← *Look back for the answers*

8

□ *You can write your answers in*

- What is the Italian for **frog**? _____

- What is the Italian for **donkey**? _____

- What is the Italian for **pig**? _____

- What is the Italian for **goose**? _____

- What is the Italian for **duck**? _____

- What is the Italian for **cow**? _____

- What is the Italian for **bull**? _____

- What is the Italian for **goat**? _____

- What is the Italian for **bird**? _____

- What is the Italian for **cat**? _____

← *Look back for the answers*

ELEMENTARY GRAMMAR

In Italian, all nouns (persons or things) are either *masculine* or *feminine*.

If they end in an *o,* they are masculine.

For example, the Italian for *bird (uccello)* and for *cat (gatto)* end in *o* and are therefore masculine words.

If the word ends in an *a,* it is a feminine word. So, *mucca* for *cow* and *oca* for *goose* are feminine words.

☐ **Now cover up the answers below:**

☐ *(You can write your answers in)*

What are the genders of these words?

porco

asino

rana

capra

_____

_____

_____

_____

_____

_____

☐ *The answers are:*

porco is *masculine*

asino is *masculine*

rana is *feminine*

capra is *feminine*

Some words do not end in *o* or *a*.

Do not worry about these words. We will deal with them later.

MORE ANIMALS

☐ **Think of each image in your mind's eye for about ten seconds**

- The Italian for **rat** is **topo.**   (TOPO)
  Imagine a rat on **top o'** a pole.

- The Italian for **wasp** is **vespa.**   (VESPA)
  Imagine a wasp making a sound like a **whisper**
  in your ear.

- The Italian for **trout** is **trota.**   (TROTA)
  Imagine a trout eating a pig's **trotter.**

- The Italian for **dog** is **cane.**   (KANAY)
  Imagine a dog chasing a **canary.**

- The Italian for **fish** is **pesce.**   (PAYSHAY)
  Imagine a **patient** in a hospital being fed a diet
  of fish.

- The Italian for **oyster** is **ostrica.**   (OSTREEKA)
  Imagine **ostriches** eating oysters.

- The Italian for **butterfly** is **farfalla.**   (FARFALLA)
  Imagine saying to a young boy who is good at
  catching butterflies, "You will go **far, fellow!**"

- The Italian for **caterpillar** is **bruco.**   (BROOKO)
  Imagine throwing caterpillars into a **brook oh!**

- The Italian for **insect** is **insetto.**   (EENSETTO)
  Imagine **insects** crawling over a plate of
  spaghetti.

- What is the English for **insetto**? _____

- What is the English for **bruco**? _____

- What is the English for **farfalla**? _____

- What is the English for **ostrica**? _____

- What is the English for **pesce**? _____

- What is the English for **cane**? _____

- What is the English for **trota**? _____

- What is the English for **vespa**? _____

- What is the English for **topo**? _____

← *Look back for the answers*

☐ *You can write your answers in*

- What is the Italian for **insect**? ————————

- What is the Italian for **caterpillar**? ————————

- What is the Italian for **butterfly**? ————————

- What is the Italian for **oyster**? ————————

- What is the Italian for **fish**? ————————

- What is the Italian for **dog**? ————————

- What is the Italian for **trout**? ————————

- What is the Italian for **wasp**? ————————

- What is the Italian for **rat**? ————————

← *Look back for the answers*

ELEMENTARY GRAMMAR

You learned after the last group of words that all nouns are either masculine or feminine. If they end in *o,* they are masculine, like *toro* for *bull.* If they end in *a,* they are feminine, like *capra* for *goat.*

If they do not end in either an *o* or an *a,* you can assume that they are masculine, although you will make the occasional mistake. Where there are exceptions in this course, we will tell you.

If the word is masculine, then the word for *the* is *il* (pronounced EEL). Imagine a man eating *eel*s!

➡ *So,*

- *il toro* is *the bull*

- *il gatto* is *the cat*

- *il topo* is *the rat*

If the word is feminine, the word for *the* is *la.*

➡ *So,*

- *la rana*   is *the frog*

- *la mucca* is *the cow*

- *la vespa* is *the wasp*

As was said just now, if the word does not end in *o* or *a,* you can assume it is masculine.

➡ *So,*

- *il cane* is *the dog*

- *il pesce* is *the fish*

☐ **Now cover up the answers below and translate the following:**

☐ *(You can write your answers in)*

1. the cat

2. the goat

3. the bull

4. the frog

5. the rat

6. the dog

7. the fish

8. the butterfly

☐ *The answers are:*

1. il gatto
2. la capra
3. il toro
4. la rana
5. il topo
6. il cane
7. il pesce
8. la farfalla

SOME MORE GRAMMAR

If a word begins with a vowel, then *the* is always *l'*—no matter what the gender.

→ *So,*

- *l'uccello* is *the bird*

- *l'oca*　　is *the goose*

- *l'anitra*　is *the duck*

- *l'insetto* is *the insect*

→ *To summarize:*

- *il*　is *masculine*

- *la* is *feminine*

If the word starts with a vowel, then *the* is *l'*—whether masculine or feminine.

ADJECTIVES—DESCRIPTION WORDS

☐ **Think of each image in your mind's eye for about ten seconds**

- The Italian for **quick** is **rapido.**   (RAPEEDO)
  Imagine being quick and **rapid.**

- The Italian for **quiet** is **tranquillo.**   (TRANKWEELLO)
  Imagine being quiet and **tranquil.**

- The Italian for **hard** is **duro.**   (DOORO)
  Imagine something hard and **durable.**

- The Italian for **fresh** is **fresco.**   (FRESKO)
  Imagine seeing a **fresco** freshly painted on a
  wall.

- The Italian for **bad** is **cattivo.**   (KATTEEVO)
  Imagine a bad cat—a **cat-evil.**

- The Italian for **empty** is **vuoto.**   (VWOTO)
  Imagine that you empty **water** from the bath.

- The Italian for **full** is **pieno.**   (PYAYNO)
  Imagine you are so full, you have to sit on a
  piano.

- The Italian for **tired** is **stanco.**   (STANKO)
  Imagine someone who was dead tired, **stank o'**
  paint.

- The Italian for **small** is **piccolo.**   (PEEKKOLO)
  Imagine a very small boy playing a **piccolo.**

- The Italian for **expensive** is **caro.**   (KARO)
  Imagine an expensive **car.**

- What is the English for **caro**?
- What is the English for **piccolo**?
- What is the English for **stanco**?
- What is the English for **pieno**?
- What is the English for **vuoto**?
- What is the English for **cattivo**?
- What is the English for **fresco**?
- What is the English for **duro**?
- What is the English for **tranquillo**?
- What is the English for **rapido**?

← *Look back for the answers*

☐ *You can write your answers in*

- What is the Italian for **expensive**? _____

- What is the Italian for **small**? _____

- What is the Italian for **tired**? _____

- What is the Italian for **full**? _____

- What is the Italian for **empty**? _____

- What is the Italian for **bad**? _____

- What is the Italian for **fresh**? _____

- What is the Italian for **hard**? _____

- What is the Italian for **quiet**? _____

- What is the Italian for **quick**? _____

← *Look back for the answers*

ELEMENTARY GRAMMAR

The Italian word for *is* is *è* (pronounced as the *e* in *hen*).

→ *So,*

- *the cat is quick* is *il gatto è rapido*

- *the rat is quick* is *il topo è rapido*

If the noun is feminine, such as *la rana* for *frog* or *la mucca* for *cow*, then the ending of the adjective changes to an *a* from an *o* to agree with the word.

If the noun is masculine, the adjective ends in *o*.

→ *So, to summarize,*

- *the cow is quick* is *la mucca è rapida*

- *the bull is quick* is *il toro è rapido*

Now cover up the answers below and translate the following:

☐ *(You can write your answers in)*

1. The bull is tired.

2. The bird is expensive.

3. The frog is quiet.

4. The fish is fresh.

5. The donkey is bad.

_____

_____

_____

_____

_____

_____

_____

_____

☐ *The answers are:*

1. Il toro è stanco.

2. L'uccello è caro.

3. La rana è tranquilla.

4. Il pesce è fresco.

5. L'asino è cattivo.

☐ **Now cover up the answers below and translate the following:**

☐ *(You can write your answers in)*

1. L'anitra è cara.

2. Il bruco è stanco.

3. Il cane è pieno.

4. L'insetto è cattivo.

5. Il porco è tranquillo.

_____

_____

_____

_____

_____

_____

_____

☐ *The answers are:*

1. The duck is expensive.

2. The caterpillar is tired.

3. The dog is full.

4. The insect is bad.

5. The pig is quiet.

SOME USEFUL ANIMAL WORDS

☐ **Think of each image in your mind's eye for about ten seconds**

- The Italian for **bee** is **ape.**   (APAY)
  Imagine a bee stinging **an ape,** or imagine a
  happy bee.
  (Note: *Ape* is a feminine word.)

- The Italian for **horse** is **cavallo.**   (KAVALLO)
  Imagine horses in the **cavalry.**

- The Italian for **jellyfish** is **medusa.**   (MEDOOZA)
  Imagine seeing what looks like a jellyfish in the
  water, but when you look closely it is **Medusa**
  with her head of snakes.

- The Italian for **fly** is **mosca.**   (MOSKA)
  Imagine **Moscow** invaded by flies.

- The Italian for **mosquito** is **zanzara.**   (DZANDZARA)
  Imagine being pestered by mosquitoes when
  you visit **Zanzibar.**

- The Italian for **chicken** is **pollo.**   (POLLO)
  Imagine using a chicken to play **polo** instead of
  a ball.

- The Italian for **sheep** is **pecora.**   (PEKORA)
  Imagine a girl asking you to **pick her a** sheep
  from the flock.

- What is the English for **pecora**? _____

- What is the English for **pollo**? _____

- What is the English for **zanzara**? _____

- What is the English for **mosca**? _____

- What is the English for **medusa**? _____

- What is the English for **cavallo**? _____

- What is the English for **ape**? _____

← *Look back for the answers*

☐ *You can write your answers in*

- What is the Italian for **sheep**? ————————

- What is the Italian for **chicken**? ————————

- What is the Italian for **mosquito**? ————————

- What is the Italian for **fly**? ————————

- What is the Italian for **jellyfish**? ————————

- What is the Italian for **horse**? ————————

- What is the Italian for **bee**? ————————

← *Look back for the answers*

ELEMENTARY GRAMMAR

When you have a noun and an adjective together like *hard pig*, *fresh fish*, then the adjective usually comes after the noun.

→ *So,*

- *the hard pig*   is *il porco duro*

- *the fresh fish*   is *il pesce fresco*

- *the bad mosquito* is *la zanzara cattiva*

☐ **Now cover up the answers below and translate the following:**

☐ *(You can write your answers in)*

1. The quick horse is quiet.

2. The tired fly is bad.

3. The expensive bird is full.

4. The small bee is empty.

5. The hard chicken is bad.

_____

_____

_____

_____

_____

_____

_____

_____

☐ *The answers are:*

1. Il cavallo rapido è tranquillo.

2. La mosca stanca è cattiva.

3. L'uccello caro è pieno.

4. L'ape piccola è vuota.

5. Il pollo duro è cattivo.

☐ **Now cover up the answers below and translate the following:**

☐ *(You can write your answers in)*

1. La mucca cattiva è piccola.

2. L'uccello rapido è caro.

3. Il topo fresco è pieno.

4. La vespa dura è vuota.

5. La trota tranquilla è stanca.

_____

_____

_____

_____

_____

_____

_____

_____

☐ *The answers are:*

1. The bad cow is small.

2. The quick bird is expensive.

3. The fresh rat is full.

4. The hard wasp is empty.

5. The quiet trout is tired.

IMPORTANT NOTE

Some of the sentences in this course might strike you as being a bit odd!

However, they have been carefully constructed to make you think much more about what you are translating. This helps the memory process and gets away from the idea of learning useful phrases "parrot fashion."

But of course, having learned with the help of these seemingly odd sentences, you can easily construct your own sentences to suit your particular needs.

SECTION 2

FURNITURE

☐ **Think of each image in your mind's eye for about ten seconds**

- The Italian for **bed** is **letto**.   (LETTO)
  Imagine a **letter** lying on your bed.

- The Italian for **table** is **tavola**.   (TAVOLA)
  Imagine wanting **to have all the** tables together.

- The Italian for **chair** is **sedia**.   (SAYDYA)
  Imagine a German who **said, "Ya,** you can sit
  on a chair."

- The Italian for **curtain** is **tenda**.   (TENDA)
  Imagine rubbing a **tender** part of your leg with
  a curtain.

- The Italian for **cushion** is **cuscino**.   (KOOSHEENO)
  Imagine a **cushion** all covered in spaghetti.

- The Italian for **cupboard** is **armadio**.   (ARMADYO)
  Imagine boats in the Spanish **armada** being
  loaded with cupboards.

- The Italian for **drawer** is **cassetto**.   (KASSETTO)
  Imagine putting your collection of **cassettes**
  in a drawer.

- The Italian for **mirror** is **specchio**.   (SPEKKYO)
  Imagine looking at the **specks you** see on a mirror.

- The Italian for **piano** is **pianoforte**.   (PYANOFORTAY)
  Imagine a **pianoforte** all covered with
  spaghetti.

- The Italian for **carpet** is **tappeto**.   (TAPPAYTO)
  Imagine having a shoe and being told to
  tap it to music on the carpet.

33

☐ *You can write your answers in*

- What is the English for **tappeto**? _____

- What is the English for **pianoforte**? _____

- What is the English for **specchio**? _____

- What is the English for **cassetto**? _____

- What is the English for **armadio**? _____

- What is the English for **cuscino**? _____

- What is the English for **tenda**? _____

- What is the English for **sedia**? _____

- What is the English for **tavola**? _____

- What is the English for **letto**? _____

← *Look back for the answers*

- What is the Italian for **carpet**? _____

- What is the Italian for **piano**? _____

- What is the Italian for **mirror**? _____

- What is the Italian for **drawer**? _____

- What is the Italian for **cupboard**? _____

- What is the Italian for **cushion**? _____

- What is the Italian for **curtain**? _____

- What is the Italian for **chair**? _____

- What is the Italian for **table**? _____

- What is the Italian for **bed**? _____

← *Look back for the answers*

ELEMENTARY GRAMMAR

There is one further point to remember about the word *the*.

You will remember that *the* is *il* when the noun is masculine (for example, *il gatto*); it is *la* if the noun is feminine (for example, *la mucca*); and if the word starts with a vowel—for example, *ape*—then the word *the* is *l'* (for example, *l'ape*).

Now, finally, if a masculine word starts with an *s* and the second letter is *not* a vowel (for example, *specchio*), then the word for *the* is *lo*.

➡ *So,*

- *the mirror* is *lo specchio*

Please do not worry about this. If you made a mistake, you would still be understood, and such words are not frequent.

PARTS OF THE HOUSE

☐ **Think of each image in your mind's eye for about ten seconds**

- The Italian for **staircase** is **scala.** (SKALA)
  Imagine **scaling** stairs, two at a time.

- The Italian for **floor** is **pavimento.** (PAVEEMENTO)
  Imagine the floor of your house is used by
  everyone as a **pavement.**

- The Italian for **kitchen** is **cucina.** (KOOCHEENA)
  Imagine keeping your **good china** in the
  kitchen.

- The Italian for **bedroom** is **camera.** (KAMAYRA)
  Imagine leaving **cameras** all over your
  bedroom.

- The Italian for **door** is **porta.** (PORTA)
  Imagine a hotel **porter** who opens the door for you.

- The Italian for **window** is **finestra.** (FEENESTRA)
  Imagine thinking "I'll **finish** painting this
  window."

- The Italian for **roof** is **tetto.** (TETTO)
  Imagine you get a **tattoo** all over you while
  sitting on your roof.

- The Italian for **room** is **stanza.** (STANTSA)
  Imagine a man **stands** in the middle of a room.

- The Italian for **bathroom** is **bagno.** (BANYO)
  Imagine they **ban you** from using your bathroom.

- The Italian for **cloakroom** is **guardaroba.** (GWARDAROBA)
  Imagine asking the attendant in a cloakroom
  to **guard a robe** that is very important.

37

□ *You can write your answers in*

- What is the English for **guardaroba**?   _____

- What is the English for **bagno**?   _____

- What is the English for **stanza**?   _____

- What is the English for **tetto**?   _____

- What is the English for **finestra**?   _____

- What is the English for **porta**?   _____

- What is the English for **camera**?   _____

- What is the English for **cucina**?   _____

- What is the English for **pavimento**?   _____

- What is the English for **scala**?   _____

← *Look back for the answers*

□ *You can write your answers in*

- What is the Italian for **cloakroom**? ———————————
- What is the Italian for **bathroom**? ———————————
- What is the Italian for **room**? ———————————
- What is the Italian for **roof**? ———————————
- What is the Italian for **window**? ———————————
- What is the Italian for **door**? ———————————
- What is the Italian for **bedroom**? ———————————
- What is the Italian for **kitchen**? ———————————
- What is the Italian for **floor**? ———————————
- What is the Italian for **staircase**? ———————————

← *Look back for the answers*

COLORS

☐ **Think of each image in your mind's eye for about ten seconds**

- The Italian for **black** is **nero.** (NAYRO)
  Imagine the Emperor **Nero** dressed all in black,
  as he throws the Christians to the lions.

- The Italian for **white** is **bianco.** (BYANKO)
  Imagine your **bank all** painted in white.

- The Italian for **blue** is **blu.** (BLOO)
  Imagine **blue** spaghetti.

- The Italian for **red** is **rosso.** (ROSSO)
  Imagine a **rose so** red, it is the color of blood.

- The Italian for **green** is **verde.** (VAIRDAY)
  Imagine the Italian composer **Verdi,** composing
  in an all-green suit.

- The Italian for **brown** is **marrone.** (MARRONAY)
  Imagine a sailor in a brown uniform **marooned**
  on a desert island.

- The Italian for **silver** is **argenteo.** (ARJENTAYO)
  Imagine sending silver to the **Argentine.**

- The Italian for **golden** is **d'oro.** (DORO)
  Imagine holding a gold **ore** in your hands.

- The Italian for **gray** is **grigio.** (GREEJO)
  Imagine someone with a gray face is waiting to
  greet you when you arrive home.

- The Italian for **yellow** is **giallo.** (JALLO)
  Imagine **yellow** spaghetti.

- What is the English for **giallo**? _____

- What is the English for **grigio**? _____

- What is the English for **d'oro**? _____

- What is the English for **argenteo**? _____

- What is the English for **marrone**? _____

- What is the English for **verde**? _____

- What is the English for **rosso**? _____

- What is the English for **blu**? _____

- What is the English for **bianco**? _____

- What is the English for **nero**? _____

← *Look back for the answers*

☐ *You can write your answers in*

- What is the Italian for **yellow**? _____

- What is the Italian for **gray**? _____

- What is the Italian for **golden**? _____

- What is the Italian for **silver**? _____

- What is the Italian for **brown**? _____

- What is the Italian for **green**? _____

- What is the Italian for **red**? _____

- What is the Italian for **blue**? _____

- What is the Italian for **white**? _____

- What is the Italian for **black**? _____

← *Look back for the answers*

☐ **Now cover up the answers below and translate the following:**

☐ *(You can write your answers in)*

1. The black drawer is empty.

2. The fresh carpet is silver.

3. The golden cushion is full.

4. The white piano is small.

5. The gray door is hard.

_____

_____

_____

_____

_____

_____

_____

_____

☐ *The answers are:*

1. Il cassetto nero è vuoto.

2. Il tappeto fresco è argenteo.

3. Il cuscino d'oro è pieno.

4. Il pianoforte bianco è piccolo.

5. La porta grigia è dura.

□ **Now cover up the answers below and translate the following:**

□ *(You can write your answers in)*

1. La camera rossa è tranquilla.

2. Il tetto d'oro è caro.

3. La finestra piccola è gialla.

4. La cucina bianca è vuota.

5. La scala nera è dura.

_____

_____

_____

_____

_____

_____

_____

_____

□ *The answers are:*

1. The red bedroom is quiet.

2. The golden roof is expensive.

3. The small window is yellow.

4. The white kitchen is empty.

5. The black stair is hard.

SOME MORE USEFUL WORDS

☐ **Think of each image in your mind's eye for about ten seconds**

- The Italian for **high** is **alto.** (ALTO)
  Imagine being at a high **altitude.**

- The Italian for **ugly** is **brutto.** (BROOTTO)
  Imagine looking at an ugly **brute.**

- The Italian for **clean** is **pulito.** (POOLEETO)
  Imagine being told **pull it to** make it clean.

- The Italian for **dirty** is **sporco.** (SPORKO)
  Imagine rubbing a dirty lamp until it **sparkles.**

- The Italian for **heavy** is **pesante.** (PAYZANTAY)
  Imagine a very heavy Italian **peasant.**

- The Italian for **low** is **basso.** (BASSO)
  Imagine a **bassoon** playing a very low note.

- The Italian for **deep** is **profondo.** (PROFOONDO)
  Imagine thinking deep, **profound** thoughts.

- The Italian for **slow** is **lento.** (LENTO)
  Imagine you do not like **lentils,** and you are
  eating them very slowly.

- The Italian for **narrow** is **stretto.** (STRETTO)
  Imagine being on the **straight** and narrow.

- The Italian for **wide** is **largo.** (LARGO)
  Imagine a football player throwing the ball wide
  after drinking too much **lager.**

- What is the English for **largo**? _____

- What is the English for **stretto**? _____

- What is the English for **lento**? _____

- What is the English for **profondo**? _____

- What is the English for **basso**? _____

- What is the English for **pesante**? _____

- What is the English for **sporco**? _____

- What is the English for **pulito**? _____

- What is the English for **brutto**? _____

- What is the English for **alto**? _____

← *Look back for the answers*

☐ *You can write your answers in*

- What is the Italian for **wide**? _____

- What is the Italian for **narrow**? _____

- What is the Italian for **slow**? _____

- What is the Italian for **deep**? _____

- What is the Italian for **low**? _____

- What is the Italian for **heavy**? _____

- What is the Italian for **dirty**? _____

- What is the Italian for **clean**? _____

- What is the Italian for **ugly**? _____

- What is the Italian for **high**? _____

← *Look back for the answers*

ELEMENTARY GRAMMAR

You will remember, from the last section, that the ending of an adjective always agrees with a noun.

➜ *For example,*

- *il tetto nero*   is *the black roof*

- *la stanza nera* is *the black room*

You will probably have noticed, however, that you have just been given some adjectives that do not end in *o* or *a*.

➜ *For example,*

- *pesante* is *heavy*

- *verde*   is *green*

When this happens, you just leave the adjective alone, whatever it goes with.

➜ *For example,*

- *the bed is green*   is *il letto è verde*

- *the table is heavy* is *la tavola è pesante*

☐ *(You can write your answers in)*

1. The red chair is dirty.

2. The black floor is ugly.

3. The yellow carpet is clean.

4. The slow pig is quiet.

5. The green curtain is heavy.

_____

_____

_____

_____

_____

_____

_____

☐ *The answers are:*

1. La sedia rossa è sporca.

2. Il pavimento nero è brutto.

3. Il tappeto giallo è pulito.

4. Il porco lento è tranquillo.

5. La tenda verde è pesante.

Now cover up the answers below and translate the following:

☐ *(You can write your answers in)*

1. La stanza blu è stretta.

2. La guardaroba verde è pulita.

3. Il bagno marrone è largo.

4. Lo specchio argenteo è sporco.

5. L'armadio blu è vuoto.

_____

_____

_____

_____

_____

_____

_____

☐ *The answers are:*

1. The blue room is narrow.

2. The green cloakroom is clean.

3. The brown bathroom is wide.

4. The silver mirror is dirty.

5. The blue cupboard is empty.

SECTION 3

CLOTHES, FAMILY WORDS

CLOTHES

☐ **Think of each image in your mind's eye for about ten seconds**

- The Italian for **hat** is **cappello.**   (KAPPELLO)
  Imagine a school **cap** in the form of a top hat.

- The Italian for **shoe** is **scarpa.**   (SKARPA)
  Imagine you **scar pa**'s shoes with a razor.

- The Italian for **trousers** or **pants** is   (PANTALONEE)
  pantaloni.
  Imagine you are wearing baggy **pantaloons**
  for trousers.

- The Italian for **skirt** is **gonna.**   (GONNA)
  Imagine telling a little girl, "That skirt is a
  goner. It has a big spot."

- The Italian for **blouse** is **blusa.**   (BLOOZA)
  Imagine wearing a **blue** blouse.

- The Italian for **shirt** is **camicia.**   (KAMEECHA)
  Imagine telling someone that "I **can meet you**
  in my shirt."

- The Italian for **dress** is **vestito.**   (VESTEETO)
  Imagine putting your **vest** on over a dress.

- The Italian for **rubber bands** is **elastico.**   (ELASTEEKO)
  Imagine a mass of **elastic** rubber bands.

- The Italian for **jacket** is **giacca.**   (JAKKA)
  Imagine you spill spaghetti all down your best
  jacket.

- The Italian for **button** is **bottone.**   (BOTTONAY)
  Imagine **buttons** cover your spaghetti.

□ *You can write your answers in*

- What is the English for **bottone**? _____

- What is the English for **giacca**? _____

- What is the English for **elastico**? _____

- What is the English for **vestito**? _____

- What is the English for **camicia**? _____

- What is the English for **blusa**? _____

- What is the English for **gonna**? _____

- What is the English for **pantaloni**? _____

- What is the English for **scarpa**? _____

- What is the English for **cappello**? _____

← *Look back for the answers*

☐ *You can write your answers in*

- What is the Italian for **button**? _____

- What is the Italian for **jacket**? _____

- What is the Italian for **rubber band**? _____

- What is the Italian for **dress**? _____

- What is the Italian for **shirt**? _____

- What is the Italian for **blouse**? _____

- What is the Italian for **skirt**? _____

- What is the Italian for **trousers**? _____

- What is the Italian for **shoe**? _____

- What is the Italian for **hat**? _____

← *Look back for the answers*

USEFUL VERBS FOR SENTENCE CONSTRUCTION

☐ **Think of each image in your mind's eye for about ten seconds**

- The Italian for **has** is **ha.** (A)
  Imagine **ah!** He *has* something.

- The Italian for **wants** is **vuole.** (VWOLAY)
  Imagine you *want* to **volley** a ball.

- The Italian for **eats** is **mangia.** (MANJA)
  Imagine someone who *eats* the restaurant
  manager.

- The Italian for **sees** is **vede.** (VAYDAY)
  Imagine you *see* a film on **video.**

☐ *You can write your answers in*

- What is the English for **vede**? _____

- What is the English for **mangia**? _____

- What is the English for **vuole**? _____

- What is the English for **ha**? _____

← *Look back for the answers*

☐ *You can write your answers in*

- What is the Italian for **sees**? _____

- What is the Italian for **eats**? _____

- What is the Italian for **wants**? _____

- What is the Italian for **has**? _____

← *Look back for the answers*

☐ **Now cover up the answers below and translate the following:**

   ☐ *(You can write your answers in)*

1. The heavy dog sees the black door.

2. The ugly horse eats the fresh goose.

3. The sheep wants the green table.

4. The red bathroom has the dirty carpet.

5. The white jellyfish eats the slow chicken.

_____

_____

_____

_____

_____

_____

_____

☐ *The answers are:*

1. Il cane pesante vede la porta nera.

2. Il cavallo brutto mangia l'oca fresca.

3. La pecora vuole la tavola verde.

4. Il bagno rosso ha il tappeto sporco.

5. La medusa bianca mangia il pollo lento.

☐ **Now cover up the answers below and translate the following:**

☐ *(You can write your answers in)*

1. Il letto duro è profondo.

2. La sedia alta è brutta.

3. La zanzara nera vede l'armadio basso.

4. La rana verde mangia l'insetto lento.

5. La trota d'oro vuole la mosca grigia.
   (*Golden* is always *d'oro,* whether after a masculine or feminine
   noun.)

_____

_____

_____

_____

_____

☐ *The answers are:*

1. The hard bed is deep.

2. The high chair is ugly.

3. The black mosquito sees the low cupboard.

4. The green frog eats the slow insect.

5. The golden trout wants the gray fly.

FAMILY WORDS

☐ **Think of each image in your mind's eye for about ten seconds**

- The Italian for **father** is **padre.**   (PADRAY)
  Imagine your father dressed up as a **padre.**

- The Italian for **mother** is (la) **madre.**   (MADRAY)
  Imagine your mother being very **mad** with you.

- The Italian for **brother** is **fratello.**   (FRATELLO)
  Imagine your brother **fraternizing** with the
  wrong crowd.

- The Italian for **sister** is **sorella.**   (SORELLA)
  Imagine your friend's sister is called Ella, and
  she is very sore at you—**sore Ella.**

- The Italian for **husband** is **marito.**   (MAREETO)
  Imagine your husband is **married to** you.

- The Italian for **wife** is (la) **moglie.**   (MOLYAY)
  Imagine that at the **mall you** see your wife.

- The Italian for **girl** is **ragazza.**   (RAGATSA)
  Imagine a whole lot of girls cheering for their
  team in a **regatta.**

- The Italian for **boy** is **ragazzo.**   (RAGATSO)
  Imagine boys cheering at a **regatta.**
  (But remember it differs from girl because it
  ends in *o.*)

- The Italian for **son** is **figlio.**   (FEELYO)
  Imagine saying to your son, who has hurt
  himself, "Let me **feel you** to see if any bones
  are broken."

- The Italian for **daughter** is **figlia.**   (FEELYA)
  Imagine saying to your daughter, who has hurt
  herself, "Let me **feel you** to see if any bones are
  broken."
  (Remember: *daughter* ends in *a.*)

You can write your answers in

- What is the English for **figlia**? _____

- What is the English for **figlio**? _____

- What is the English for **ragazzo**? _____

- What is the English for **ragazza**? _____

- What is the English for **moglie**? _____

- What is the English for **marito**? _____

- What is the English for **sorella**? _____

- What is the English for **fratello**? _____

- What is the English for **madre**? _____

- What is the English for **padre**? _____

← *Look back for the answers*

- What is the Italian for **daughter**?   ——————————

- What is the Italian for **son**?   ——————————

- What is the Italian for **boy**?   ——————————

- What is the Italian for **girl**?   ——————————

- What is the Italian for **wife**?   ——————————

- What is the Italian for **husband**?   ——————————

- What is the Italian for **sister**?   ——————————

- What is the Italian for **brother**?   ——————————

- What is the Italian for **mother**?   ——————————

- What is the Italian for **father**?   ——————————

← *Look back for the answers*

SOME MORE USEFUL WORDS

☐ **Think of each image in your mind's eye for about ten seconds**

- The Italian for **yes** is **sì**.   (SEE)
  Imagine you **see** the answer must be *yes*.

- The Italian for **no** is **no**.   (NO)
  Imagine shouting "Please, **no** spaghetti!"

- The Italian for **not** is **non**.   (NON)
  Imagine thinking "I am *not* a **non**-person."

- The Italian for **very** is **molto**.   (MOLTO)
  Imagine **molten** lead is *very* hot.

- The Italian for **only** is **solo**.   (SOLO)
  Imagine thinking "I am the *only* one going—
  I am going **solo**."

☐ *You can write your answers in*

- What is the English for **solo**? _____

- What is the English for **molto**? _____

- What is the English for **non**? _____

- What is the English for **no**? _____

- What is the English for **sì**? _____

← *Look back for the answers*

☐ *You can write your answers in*

- What is the Italian for **only**?   _____

- What is the Italian for **very**?   _____

- What is the Italian for **not**?   _____

- What is the Italian for **no**?   _____

- What is the Italian for **yes**?   _____

← *Look back for the answers*

ELEMENTARY GRAMMAR

In this section, you will be shown how to use the words *and, but,* and *or.*

☐   The Italian for *and* is *e*. (The *e* sounds like *a* in *hay.*) Imagine *hay* and straw.

➜   *For example,*

• *the dog and the cat* is *il cane e il gatto*

(Remember, the Italian for *is* is *è*, and it sounds like the *e* in *hen.*)

☐   The Italian for *but* is *ma*. Imagine saying "But, *Ma*, he's making eyes at me!"

➜   *For example,*

• *expensive but bad* is *caro ma cattivo*

☐   The Italian for *or* is *o*.

   O is the first letter of the word *or*—it is as if the Italians have forgotten to put the *r* on the word.

➜   *For example,*

• *red or black* is *rosso o nero*

Now cover up the answers below and translate the following:

☐ *(You can write your answers in)*

1. The father wants the black dog, but the mother wants the white cat.

2. Yes, the son is very heavy and very clean.

3. No, the wife is not ugly.

4. Only the hat is very dirty.

5. The boy has the red shirt and the girl has the green dress.

_____

_____

_____

_____

_____

_____

_____

_____

☐ *The answers are:*

1. Il padre vuole il cane nero, ma la madre vuole il gatto bianco.

2. Sì, il figlio è molto pesante e molto pulito.

3. No, la moglie non è brutta.

4. Solo il cappello è molto sporco.

5. Il ragazzo ha la camicia rossa e la ragazza ha il vestito verde.

Now cover up the answers below and translate the following:

☐ *(You can write your answers in)*

1. La ragazza è sporca, o il ragazzo è pulito.

2. No, solo la scarpa è pesante.

3. Il bottone è molto brutto, e il vestito è molto piccolo.

4. La giacca sporca è verde e marrone, ma non bianca.

5. Il cavallo ha la scarpa rossa, e il gatto vuole la blusa cara.

_____

_____

_____

_____

_____

_____

_____

_____

☐ *The answers are:*

1. The girl is dirty, or the boy is clean.
2. No, only the shoe is heavy.
3. The button is very ugly, and the dress is very small.
4. The dirty jacket is green and brown, but not white.
5. The horse has the red shoe, and the cat wants the expensive blouse.

ELEMENTARY GRAMMAR

The Italian for *a* as in *a pig* or *an animal* is *un* (which sounds like OON).

➜ *For example,*

- *a pig*   is *un porco*

- *an animal* is *un animale*

Where the word is feminine, as in *a cow* or *a table,* then the word for *a* is:

una

In other words, you add the feminine ending *a* to *un*.

➜ *For example,*

- *a cow* is *una mucca*

- *a table* is *una tavola*

(Where a feminine word starts with a vowel—for example, *ape* for *bee*—then the word for *a* is *un',* which sounds like the masculine form of *a . . . un.*)

☐ *(You can write your answers in)*

1. A red chair is very dirty.

2. The brother eats an expensive chicken.

3. The sister wants a clean skirt.

4. The yellow jellyfish has a red fish.

5. A blue blouse is very dirty.

_____

_____

_____

_____

_____

_____

_____

_____

☐ *The answers are:*

1. Una sedia rossa è molto sporca.

2. Il fratello mangia un pollo caro.

3. La sorella vuole una gonna pulita.

4. La medusa gialla ha un pesce rosso.

5. Una blusa blu è molto sporca.

☐ **Now cover up the answers below and translate the following:**

☐ *(You can write your answers in)*

1. Il marito ha un cavallo molto cattivo, ma la moglie ha un'ape piccola.

2. Sì, la sorella vuole una camicia rossa.

3. Il figlio vede una blusa verde, ma la figlia vede una giacca molto nera.

4. Solo il bottone è caro.

5. No, l'elastico non è duro.

_____

_____

_____

_____

_____

_____

☐ *The answers are:*

1. The husband has a very bad horse, but the wife has a small bee.

2. Yes, the sister wants a red shirt.

3. The son sees a green blouse, but the daughter sees a very black jacket.

4. Only the button is expensive.

5. No, the rubber band is not hard.

SECTION 4

IN THE COUNTRY, TIME WORDS

COUNTRY WORDS

☐ **Think of each image in your mind's eye for about ten seconds**

- The Italian for **garden** is **giardino.** (JARDEENO)
  Imagine your elbow being **jarred in** the garden.

- The Italian for **flower** is **fiore.** (FYORAY)
  Imagine you are in a **fury** when your dog digs
  up your flowers.

- The Italian for **tree** is **albero.** (ALBERO)
  Imagine someone saying, "**I'll bare all** if you
  cut this tree down."

- The Italian for **plant** is **pianta.** (PYANTA)
  Imagine wrapping a plant in a pair of **pants.**

- The Italian for **grass** is **erba.** (AIRBA)
  Imagine using **herbs** and grass to season your
  food.

- The Italian for **path** is **sentiero.** (SENTYAIRO)
  Imagine a path running through the **center** of
  your garden.

- The Italian for **fruit** is **frutta.** (FROOTTA)
  Imagine **fruit** all covered with spaghetti.

You can write your answers in

- What is the English for **frutta**?   _____

- What is the English for **sentiero**?   _____

- What is the English for **erba**?   _____

- What is the English for **pianta**?   _____

- What is the English for **albero**?   _____

- What is the English for **fiore**?   _____

- What is the English for **giardino**?   _____

← *Look back for the answers*

- What is the Italian for **fruit**?   _____

- What is the Italian for **path**?   _____

- What is the Italian for **grass**?   _____

- What is the Italian for **plant**?   _____

- What is the Italian for **tree**?   _____

- What is the Italian for **flower**?   _____

- What is the Italian for **garden**?   _____

← *Look back for the answers*

TIME

☐ **Think of each image in your mind's eye for about ten seconds**

- The Italian for **time** is **tempo**.   (TEMPO)
  Imagine keeping time to the **tempo** of the
  music.

- The Italian for **second** is **secondo**.   (SEKONDO)
  Imagine a piece of spaghetti swinging like a
  pendulum every **second**.

- The Italian for **minute** is **minuto**.   (MEENOOTO)
  Imagine trying to eat a plate full of spaghetti
  in under a **minute**.

- The Italian for **hour** is **ora**.   (ORA)
  Imagine waiting in **horror** for the hour to
  strike.

- The Italian for **week** is **settimana**.   (SETTEEMANA)
  Imagine you visit the city only once a week
  because you are not a **city man—ah!**

- The Italian for **month** is **mese**.   (MAYZAY)
  Imagine being lost in a **maze** for a month.

- The Italian for **year** is **anno**.   (ANNO)
  Imagine an **annual** event takes place once a
  year.

- The Italian for **day** is **giorno**.   (JORNO)
  Imagine a long **journey** that takes you all day.

- The Italian for **night** is (la) **notte**.   (NOTTAY)
  Imagine the children being **naughty** all night.

- The Italian for **tomorrow** is **domani**.   (DOMANEE)
  Imagine agreeing to play someone at **dominoes**
  tomorrow.

- What is the English for **domani**? _____

- What is the English for (la) **notte**? _____

- What is the English for **giorno**? _____

- What is the English for **anno**? _____

- What is the English for **mese**? _____

- What is the English for **settimana**? _____

- What is the English for **ora**? _____

- What is the English for **minuto**? _____

- What is the English for **secondo**? _____

- What is the English for **tempo**? _____

← *Look back for the answers*

☐ *You can write your answers in*

- What is the Italian for **tomorrow**? _____

- What is the Italian for **night**? _____

- What is the Italian for **day**? _____

- What is the Italian for **year**? _____

- What is the Italian for **month**? _____

- What is the Italian for **week**? _____

- What is the Italian for **hour**? _____

- What is the Italian for **minute**? _____

- What is the Italian for **second**? _____

- What is the Italian for **time**? _____

← *Look back for the answers*

SOME MORE USEFUL WORDS

☐ **Think of each image in your mind's eye for about ten seconds**

- The Italian for **more** is **più.** (PYOO)
  Imagine there being *more* people than a church **pew** can hold.

- The Italian for **soon** is **presto.** (PRESTO)
  Imagine thinking "Hey **presto!** I'll *soon* be rich!"

- The Italian for **always** is **sempre.** (SEMPRAY)
  Imagine someone who *always* **simpers.**

- The Italian for **less** is **meno.** (MAYNO)
  Imagine you have never seen a **menu** with *less* on it.

- The Italian for **now** is **adesso.** (ADESSO)
  Imagine someone demanding your **address** *now.*

- The Italian for **every** is **ogni.** (ONYEE)
  Imagine **onions** with *every* meal in your hotel.

☐ *You can write your answers in*

- What is the English for **ogni**?   _____

- What is the English for **adesso**?   _____

- What is the English for **meno**?   _____

- What is the English for **sempre**?   _____

- What is the English for **presto**?   _____

- What is the English for **più**?   _____

← *Look back for the answers*

☐ *You can write your answers in*

- What is the Italian for **every**?   _____

- What is the Italian for **now**?   _____

- What is the Italian for **less**?   _____

- What is the Italian for **always**?   _____

- What is the Italian for **soon**?   _____

- What is the Italian for **more**?   _____

← *Look back for the answers*

☐ **Now cover up the answers below and translate the following:**

☐ *(You can write your answers in)*

1. The dog eats the grass now.

2. The father wants less white fish.

3. The mother eats more fruit.

4. The plant is always clean, but the tree is always dirty.

5. The daughter wants a garden soon or a flower.

_____

_____

_____

_____

_____

_____

_____

☐ *The answers are:*

1. Il cane mangia l'erba adesso.

2. Il padre vuole meno pesce bianco.

3. La madre mangia più frutta.

4. La pianta è sempre pulita, ma l'albero è sempre sporco.

5. La figlia vuole un giardino presto o un fiore.

☐ **Now cover up the answers below and translate the following:**

☐ *(You can write your answers in)*

1. La pianta è sempre nera.

2. La mucca vuole più frutta e meno erba.

3. La trota mangia la mosca adesso.

4. Presto la notte è giorno.

5. Il topo vede un sentiero adesso.

_____

_____

_____

_____

_____

_____

_____

_____

☐ *The answers are:*

1. The plant is always black.

2. The cow wants more fruit and less grass.

3. The trout eats the fly now.

4. Soon the night is day.

5. The rat sees a path now.

DAYS OF THE WEEK

□ **Think of each image in your mind's eye for about ten seconds**

- The Italian for **Monday** is **lunedì.**   (LOONAYDEE)
  Imagine Monday being a **loony day.**

- The Italian for **Tuesday** is **martedì.**   (MARTAYDEE)
  Imagine **martyrs** being burned on Tuesdays.

- The Italian for **Wednesday** is **mercoledì.**   (MAIRKOLAYDEE)
  Imagine a **miracle lady** passes your door
  every Wednesday.

- The Italian for **Thursday** is **giovedì.**   (JOVAYDEE)
  Imagine Thursday being a **jovial day.**

- The Italian for **Friday** is **venerdì.**   (VENAIRDEE)
  Imagine putting a **veneer** on some wood every
  Friday when you come home from work.

- The Italian for **Saturday** is **sabato.**   (SABATO)
  Imagine Saturday being the Jewish **Sabbath.**

- The Italian for **Sunday** is **domenica.**   (DOMAYNEEKA)
  Imagine **Dominican** monks praying
  on Sunday.

☐ *You can write your answers in*

- What is the English for **domenica**?   _____

- What is the English for **sabato**?   _____

- What is the English for **venerdì**?   _____

- What is the English for **giovedì**?   _____

- What is the English for **mercoledì**?   _____

- What is the English for **martedì**?   _____

- What is the English for **lunedì**?   _____

← *Look back for the answers*

☐ *You can write your answers in*

- What is the Italian for **Sunday**?   _____

- What is the Italian for **Saturday**?   _____

- What is the Italian for **Friday**?   _____

- What is the Italian for **Thursday**?   _____

- What is the Italian for **Wednesday**?   _____

- What is the Italian for **Tuesday**?   _____

- What is the Italian for **Monday**?   _____

← *Look back for the answers*

ELEMENTARY GRAMMAR

The way to ask questions in Italian when you are speaking is by *tone of voice*.

You do not change the word order.

➔ *For example,*

- *È un toro?* is *Is it a bull?*

In Italian, there is no need to use the word *it, I, he,* etc., with a verb.

➔ *So,*

- *It is a bull*   is *È un toro*

- *He wants a bull*   is *Vuole un toro*

- *Does he want a bull?* is *Vuole un toro?*

Remember, a question is asked by tone of voice—not by changing the word order.

☐ *(You can write your answers in)*

1. It is a flower.

2. Is it an hour or is it a day?

3. Is he an ugly boy?

4. She is an ugly girl.

5. Does she have a green garden and a brown path?

_____

_____

_____

_____

_____

_____

_____

_____

☐ *The answers are:*

1. È un fiore.

2. È un'ora o è un giorno?

3. È un ragazzo brutto?

4. È una ragazza brutta.

5. Ha un giardino verde e un sentiero marrone?

☐ **Now cover up the answers below and translate the following:**

☐ *(You can write your answers in)*

1. È lunedì o martedì domani?

2. È un mese cattivo e un anno cattivo?

3. È un secondo rapido ma un minuto lento.

4. Ogni settimana ha un mercoledì, un giovedì, un venerdì, un sabato, e una domenica.

5. È la notte adesso.

_____

_____

_____

_____

_____

_____

☐ *The answers are:*

1. Is it Monday or Tuesday tomorrow?

2. Is it a bad month and a bad year?

3. It is a quick second but a slow minute.

4. Every week has a Wednesday, a Thursday, a Friday, a Saturday, and a Sunday.

5. It is the night now.

SECTION 5

RESTAURANT, NUMBERS, TELLING TIME, FOOD AND DRINK

IN A RESTAURANT

☐ **Think of each image in your mind's eye for about ten seconds**

- The Italian for **restaurant** is **ristorante.**   (REESTORANTAY)
  Imagine a **restaurant** that sells spaghetti
  with everything.

- The Italian for **waiter** is **cameriere.**   (KAMAIRYAIRAY)
  Imagine a waiter with a **camera** slung
  round his neck.
  (Don't confuse with *camera*—bedroom.)

- The Italian for **bill** is **conto.**   (KONTO)
  Imagine **counting** your bill.

- The Italian for **cup** is **tazza.**   (TATSA)
  Imagine a **tassel** dangling from the handle of your cup.

- The Italian for **plate** is **piatto.**   (PYATTO)
  Imagine someone telling you, "**Be at home.**
  Throw plates around."

- The Italian for **knife** is **coltello.**   (KOLTELLO)
  Imagine wrapping a knife in a **cold towel.**

- The Italian for **fork** is **forchetta.**   (FORKETTA)
  Imagine telling a child not to **forget a** fork when eating.

- The Italian for **spoon** is **cucchiaio.**   (KOOKYAYO)
  Imagine saying to someone, "A **cookie I owe**
  you for the silver spoon you gave me."

- The Italian for **menu** is **menu.**   (MENOO)
  Imagine a **menu** that has spaghetti with everything.

- The Italian for **glass** is **bicchiere.**   (BEEKYAIRAY)
  Imagine being given a laboratory **beaker**
  instead of a glass when you ask for a glass.

☐ *You can write your answers in*

- What is the English for **bicchiere**?   _____

- What is the English for **menu**?   _____

- What is the English for **cucchiaio**?   _____

- What is the English for **forchetta**?   _____

- What is the English for **coltello**?   _____

- What is the English for **piatto**?   _____

- What is the English for **tazza**?   _____

- What is the English for **conto**?   _____

- What is the English for **cameriere**?   _____

- What is the English for **ristorante**?   _____

← *Look back for the answers*

☐ *You can write your answers in*

- What is the Italian for **glass**? ───────────

- What is the Italian for **menu**? ───────────

- What is the Italian for **spoon**? ───────────

- What is the Italian for **fork**? ───────────

- What is the Italian for **knife**? ───────────

- What is the Italian for **plate**? ───────────

- What is the Italian for **cup**? ───────────

- What is the Italian for **bill**? ───────────

- What is the Italian for **waiter**? ───────────

- What is the Italian for **restaurant**? ───────────

← *Look back for the answers*

NUMBERS

☐ **Think of each image in your mind's eye for about ten seconds**

- The Italian for **one** is **uno**.　　　　　(OONO)
  Imagine **you know** one when you see it.

- The Italian for **two** is **due**.　　　　　(DOOAY)
  Imagine a **duo,** two people, singing.

- The Italian for **three** is **tre**.　　　　　(TRAY)
  Imagine three **trays.**

- The Italian for **four** is **quattro**.　　　(KWATTRO)
  Imagine four **quarters.**

- The Italian for **five** is **cinque**.　　　(CHEENKWAY)
  Imagine the **chink** of five coins.

- The Italian for **six** is **sei**.　　　　　(SAY)
  Imagine you **say** six, six times in Italian: say,
  say, say, say, say, say.

- The Italian for **seven** is **sette**.　　　(SETTAY)
  Imagine you have seven **settees,** one for each
  day of the week.

- The Italian for **eight** is **otto**.　　　　(OTTO)
  Imagine **Otto** the octopus, with eight legs.

- The Italian for **nine** is **nove**.　　　　(NOVAY)
  Imagine a German shouting "Nein! There is **no
  vay** the U.S. will score nine goals against
  Germany."

- The Italian for **zero** is **zero**.　　　　(DZAYRO)
  Imagine there is no spaghetti, the supply is
  down to **zero.**

☐ *You can write your answers in*

- What is the English for **zero**? _____

- What is the English for **nove**? _____

- What is the English for **otto**? _____

- What is the English for **sette**? _____

- What is the English for **sei**? _____

- What is the English for **cinque**? _____

- What is the English for **quattro**? _____

- What is the English for **tre**? _____

- What is the English for **due**? _____

- What is the English for **uno**? _____

← *Look back for the answers*

☐ *You can write your answers in*

- What is the Italian for **zero**? _____

- What is the Italian for **nine**? _____

- What is the Italian for **eight**? _____

- What is the Italian for **seven**? _____

- What is the Italian for **six**? _____

- What is the Italian for **five**? _____

- What is the Italian for **four**? _____

- What is the Italian for **three**? _____

- What is the Italian for **two**? _____

- What is the Italian for **one**? _____

← *Look back for the answers*

ELEMENTARY GRAMMAR

While plurals in Italian are usually very simple, it is best to treat the plurals for masculine and feminine nouns separately.

Masculine Plurals

All masculine nouns, almost without exception, end in *i* (pronounced EE) in the plural.

➜ *For example,*

- *topo* (rat)　　becomes *topi* (rats)

- *fiore* (flower) becomes *fiori* (flowers)

The word for *the* becomes *i* (pronounced EE) in the plural.

➜ *For example,*

- *il toro* (the bull)　　becomes *i tori* (the bulls)

- *il cameriere* (the waiter) becomes *i camerieri* (the waiters)

You will remember that where a word starts with a vowel, for example, *albero,* the word for *the* is *l'.*

➜ *So,*

- *the tree* is *l'albero*

- *the bird* is *l'uccello*

For these words, the word for *the* becomes *gli* (pronounced like LEE) in the plural. For example,

- *l'uccello* (the bird) becomes *gli uccelli* (the birds)

- *l'albero* (the tree)　becomes *gli alberi* (the trees)

☐ **Now cover up the answers below and translate the following:**

☐ *(You can write your answers in)*

1. The boy has two brothers.

2. The bird eats the chickens every day.

3. The husband wants four knives, three plates, and six glasses.

4. The son sees the birds.

5. The wife wants nine flowers.

_____

_____

_____

_____

_____

_____

_____

_____

☐ *The answers are:*

1. Il ragazzo ha due fratelli.

2. L'uccello mangia i polli ogni giorno.

3. Il marito vuole quattro coltelli, tre piatti, e sei bicchieri.

4. Il figlio vede gli uccelli.

5. La moglie vuole nove fiori.

□ **Now cover up the answers below and translate the following:**

□ *(You can write your answers in)*

1. Il ragazzo ha otto conti, e la ragazza vuole due conti.

2. Il figlio vede i due coltelli.

3. Il cameriere vuole quattro piatti, tre forchette, e i cinque bicchieri.

4. La sorella vede gli asini, e la madre vede gli alberi, ma il fratello non vede gli uccelli.

5. Il bruco ha i nove giardini.

_____

_____

_____

_____

_____

_____

□ *The answers are:*

1. The boy has eight bills, and the girl wants two bills.

2. The son sees the two knives.

3. The waiter wants four plates, three forks, and the five glasses.

4. The sister sees the donkeys, and the mother sees the trees, but the brother does not see the birds.

5. The caterpillar has the nine gardens.

ELEMENTARY GRAMMAR

Feminine Plurals

Again, feminine plurals are straightforward.

All feminine nouns ending in *a* change to *e*.

➔ *For example,*

- *forchetta* (fork) becomes *forchette* (forks)

- *sorella* (sister) becomes *sorelle* (sisters)

The word for *the* in the plural is always *le,* whether the word starts with a vowel or not.

➔ *For example,*

- *la rana* (the frog) becomes *le rane* (the frogs)

- *l'ora* (the hour) becomes *le ore* (the hours)

The rules that you have been given cover the great majority of words. Occasionally you will make mistakes because there are exceptions.

☐ **Now cover up the answers below and translate the following:**

☐ *(You can write your answers in)*

1. The duck eats six frogs.

2. The girl has eight hours.

3. The sister wants the tables and the chairs.

4. The cat has two shoes and five cups.

5. The mother wants four plates and seven skirts.

_____

_____

_____

_____

_____

_____

_____

☐ *The answers are:*

1. L'anitra mangia sei rane.
2. La ragazza ha otto ore.
3. La sorella vuole le tavole e le sedie.
4. Il gatto ha due scarpe e cinque tazze.
5. La madre vuole quattro piatti e sette gonne.

☐ **Now cover up the answers below and translate the following:**

    ☐ *(You can write your answers in)*

1.   Il cameriere vuole le due piante.

2.   Il marito ha le quattro tende, le cinque porte, e le otto sedie, ma non le tre finestre o le due tavole.

3.   Il gatto vede le erbe, i cassetti, e le finestre.

4.   La rana vede la frutta.

5.   Vede il cavallo e le scale.

_____

_____

_____

_____

_____

_____

☐ *The answers are:*

1.   The waiter wants the two plants.

2.   The husband has the four curtains, the five doors, and the eight chairs, but not the three windows or the two tables.

3.   The cat sees the grasses, the drawers, and the windows.

4.   The frog sees the fruit.

5.   He (*or* She) sees the horse and the stairs.

FOOD AND DRINK

☐ **Think of each image in your mind's eye for about ten seconds**

- The Italian for **bread** is **pane.**   (PANAY)
  Imagine a **pan** full of bread.

- The Italian for **butter** is **burro.**   (BOORRO)
  Imagine a writing **bureau** smeared with butter.

- The Italian for **wine** is **vino.**   (VEENO)
  Imagine a German saying, "**Ve know** what the
  best wine is."

- The Italian for **water** is **acqua.**   (AKWA)
  Imagine an **aqueduct** bringing water to your
  hotel.

- The Italian for **milk** is **latte.**   (LATTAY)
  Imagine a **Latin** teacher drinking milk while
  reciting Latin verbs.

- The Italian for **salt** is **sale.**   (SALAY)
  Imagine sprinkling salt on your **salad.**

- The Italian for **pepper** is **pepe.**   (PAYPAY)
  Imagine someone demanding **Pay! Pay!** for the
  pepper you have used.

- The Italian for **coffee** is **caffè.**   (KAFFE)
  Imagine drinking coffee in a **café.**

- The Italian for **tea** is **tè.**   (TE)
  Imagine pouring **tea** all over your spaghetti.

- The Italian for **jam** is **marmellata.**   (MARMELLATA)
  Imagine mixing jam and **marmalade** on
  your bread.

☐ *You can write your answers in*

- What is the English for **marmellata**? _____

- What is the English for **tè**? _____

- What is the English for **caffè**? _____

- What is the English for **pepe**? _____

- What is the English for **sale**? _____

- What is the English for **latte**? _____

- What is the English for **acqua**? _____

- What is the English for **vino**? _____

- What is the English for **burro**? _____

- What is the English for **pane**? _____

← *Look back for the answers*

☐ *You can write your answers in*

- What is the Italian for **jam**?   _____

- What is the Italian for **tea**?   _____

- What is the Italian for **coffee**?   _____

- What is the Italian for **pepper**?   _____

- What is the Italian for **salt**?   _____

- What is the Italian for **milk**?   _____

- What is the Italian for **water**?   _____

- What is the Italian for **wine**?   _____

- What is the Italian for **butter**?   _____

- What is the Italian for **bread**?   _____

← *Look back for the answers*

ELEMENTARY GRAMMAR

Adjectives also become plural in Italian, and they change their endings to agree with the word they go with.

(This is exactly the same kind of thing that is done in the singular, where an adjective has to agree with the noun.)

➤ *For example,*

- *black dogs* is *cani neri*

- *black frogs* is *rane nere*

Where an adjective already ends in an *e*, for example, *verde* (*green*), then it changes to end in an *i* (*verdi*) no matter what the gender of the noun.

➤ *So,*

- *green dogs* is *cani verdi*

- *green frogs* is *rane verdi*

Finally, the word for *are* is *sono*. Imagine asking if you are the *son o'* your father.

➤ *For example,*

- *The dogs are heavy* is *I cani sono pesanti*

- *The tables are ugly* is *Le tavole sono brutte*

Sometimes one word is masculine and the other feminine, for example:

- The dog and the frog are black

Then the adjective takes the *masculine* form:

- *Il cane e la rana sono neri*

□ **Now cover up the answers below and translate the following:**

□ *(You can write your answers in)*

1. The restaurants are empty.

2. The glasses are full.

3. The chairs are high.

4. The beds are very clean.

5. Are the waiters quick?

_____

_____

_____

_____

_____

_____

_____

_____

□ *The answers are:*

1. I ristoranti sono vuoti.

2. I bicchieri sono pieni.

3. Le sedie sono alte.

4. I letti sono molto puliti.

5. I camerieri sono rapidi?

☐ Now cover up the answers below and translate the following:

☐ *(You can write your answers in)*

1. Adesso l'acqua, le tazze strette, e i piatti profondi sono verdi.

2. Il menu è caro ogni giorno ma il pane e il latte sono freschi.
   (*Freschi* is pronounced FRESKEE.)

3. Il caffè e il tè sono puliti, ma il pepe e la marmellata sono sporchi.
   (*Sporchi* is pronounced SPORKEE.)

4. Il vino e la forchetta sono pesanti.

5. Mangia il burro e il pane duro.

_____

_____

_____

_____

_____

☐ *The answers are:*

1. Now the water, the narrow cups, and the deep plates are green.

2. The menu is expensive every day, but the bread and the milk are fresh.

3. The coffee and the tea are clean, but the pepper and the jam are dirty.

4. The wine and the fork are heavy.

5. He (or she or it) eats the butter and the hard bread.

TELLING TIME (1)

☐ **Think of each image in your mind's eye for about ten seconds**

The next part of Section 5 deals with telling the time. However, first you will need to know some more numbers and words.

- The Italian for **ten** is **dieci.** (DYAYCHEE)
  Imagine a **diet sheet** with ten colors for different food items.

- The Italian for **eleven** is **undici.** (OONDEECHEE)
  Imagine punching eleven football players **on the chin.**

- The Italian for **noon** (midday) is **mezzogiorno.** (MEDZOJORNO)
  Imagine an Italian **made the journey** at noon.

- The Italian for **midnight** is **mezzanotte.** (MEDZANOTTAY)
  Imagine an Italian waiter **made ze naughty** suggestion at midnight.

- The Italian for **quarter** is **quarto.** (KWARTO)
  Imagine cutting your spaghetti into **quarters.**

- The Italian for **half** is **mezzo.** (MEDZO)
  Imagine the **Med's so** dirty half the population will not swim in it. (A **mezzo** soprano is half a soprano.)

- The Italian for **twenty** is **venti.** (VENTEE)
  Imagine an air conditioner with twenty **vents.**

- The Italian for **twenty-five** is **venticinque.** (VENTEECHEENKWAY)
  Imagine you add twenty and five together.
  (*Venti* and *cinque*)

☐ *You can write your answers in*

- What is the English for **venticinque**? _____

- What is the English for **venti**? _____

- What is the English for **mezzo**? _____

- What is the English for **quarto**? _____

- What is the English for **mezzogiorno**? _____

- What is the English for **mezzanotte**? _____

- What is the English for **undici**? _____

- What is the English for **dieci**? _____

← *Look back for the answers*

You can write your answers in

- What is the Italian for **twenty-five**?   _____

- What is the Italian for **twenty**?   _____

- What is the Italian for **half**?   _____

- What is the Italian for **quarter**?   _____

- What is the Italian for **midnight**?   _____

- What is the Italian for **noon**?   _____

- What is the Italian for **eleven**?   _____

- What is the Italian for **ten**?   _____

← *Look back for the answers*

TELLING TIME (2)

As you learned earlier, the Italian for *the hour* is *l'ora,* which is of course feminine. The Italian for *what* is *che* (pronounced KAY).

The Italian for *What time is it?* is *Che ora è?* (What hour is?).

To answer this question in Italian with, for example, *It's one o'clock, two o'clock,* etc., the literal translation is *It is the one, they are the two, they are the three.*

The word for *hour* is not said but is understood.

➜ *So,*

- *It is one o'clock* is *It is the one*
  È l'una

- *It is two o'clock* is *They are the two*
  Sono le due

Remember that the word for *the* is feminine because the word for *hour* is feminine.

- *It is three o'clock*   is *They are the three*
  Sono le tre

- *It is eleven o'clock* is *They are the eleven*
  Sono le undici

☐ **Now cover up the answers below and translate the following:**

☐ *(You can write your answers in)*

1. It is five o'clock.

2. It is three o'clock.

3. It is seven o'clock.

4. It is four o'clock.

5. It is one o'clock.

_____

_____

_____

_____

_____

_____

_____

☐ *The answers are:*

1. Sono le cinque.

2. Sono le tre.

3. Sono le sette.

4. Sono le quattro.

5. È l'una.

TELLING TIME (3)

To say *it is midnight* or *noon (midday),* you simply say:

- *È mezzanotte* (It is midnight)

- *È mezzogiorno* (It is noon)

Do not use the word *the*.

When you want to say *It is five after seven* or *ten after eight*, etc., then you say *They are seven and five*, etc.

➜ *So,*

- *It is five after three*   is *They are the three and five*
                                  Sono le tre e cinque

- *It is ten after ten*   is *They are the ten and ten*
                                  Sono le dieci e dieci

- *It is half past six*   is *They are the six and half*
                                  Sono le sei e mezzo

- *It is quarter after six* is *They are the six and a quarter*
                                  Sono le sei e un quarto

□ **Now cover up the answers below and translate the following:**

□ *(You can write your answers in)*

1. It is ten after four.

2. It is five after nine.

3. It is half past three.

4. It is quarter after eight.

5. It is quarter after six.

_____

_____

_____

_____

_____

_____

_____

_____

□ *The answers are:*

1. Sono le quattro e dieci.

2. Sono le nove e cinque.

3. Sono le tre e mezzo.

4. Sono le otto e un quarto.

5. Sono le sei e un quarto.

TELLING TIME (4)

When you want to say *It is ten to four* or *twenty to four,* then in Italian you say *They are four minus twenty.*

In Italian, this is *Sono le quattro meno venti.*

➔ *So,*

- *It is five to three*   is *They are the three minus five*
  Sono le tre meno cinque

- *It is a quarter to eight* is *They are the eight minus a quarter*
  Sono le otto meno un quarto

Remember, if it is *quarter to one,* then you say *È l'una meno un quarto.*

☐ **Now cover up the answers below and translate the following:**

☐ *(You can write your answers in)*

1. It is quarter to four.

2. It is quarter after twelve (midnight).

3. It is twenty-five to three.

4. It is twenty after twelve (noon).

5. It is ten to seven.

6. It is five to eleven.

7. It is half past three.

8. It is half past one.

_____

_____

_____

☐ *The answers are:*

1. Sono le quattro meno un quarto.

2. È mezzanotte e un quarto.

3. Sono le tre meno venticinque.

4. È mezzogiorno e venti.

5. Sono le sette meno dieci.

6. Sono le undici meno cinque.

7. Sono le tre e mezzo.

8. È l'una e mezzo.

Please note: To say *at 2 o'clock,* you simply say *alle due.*

- *At half past six* is *Alle sei e mezzo*

- *At noon*   is *A mezzogiorno,* etc.

(*A* and *alle* will be dealt with more fully later on.)

SECTION 6

MORE FOOD AND DRINK

SOME FOODS

☐ **Think of each image in your mind's eye for about ten seconds**

- The Italian for **soup** is **minestra.**   (MEENESTRA)
  Imagine **minestrone** soup.

- The Italian for **meat** is (la) **carne.**   (KARNAY)
  Imagine **carnivores** eating meat.

- The Italian for **lamb** is **agnello.**   (ANYELLO)
  Imagine **an all-yellow** lamb.

- The Italian for **steak** is **bistecca.**   (BEESTEKKA)
  Imagine asking for a **beefsteak** and spaghetti.

- The Italian for **pea** is **pisello.**   (PEEZELLO)
  Imagine meeting a can of peas for the first time
  and saying, "**Peas hello.**"

- The Italian for **garlic** is **aglio.**   (ALYO)
  Imagine thinking that **all you** need to put
  someone off is to eat garlic.

- The Italian for **carrot** is **carota.**   (KAROTA)
  Imagine spaghetti and **carrots.**

- The Italian for **cabbage** is **cavolo.**   (KAVOLO)
  Imagine throwing cabbage at a charging
  cavalry.

- The Italian for **onion** is **cipolla.**   (CHEEPOLLA)
  Imagine that the onions are so inexpensive you
  say, "They are **cheapola.**"

- The Italian for **mushroom** is **fungo.**   (FOONGO)
  Imagine that the **fungus** that you collect are all
  edible mushrooms.

☐ *You can write your answers in*

- What is the English for **fungo**? _____

- What is the English for **cipolla**? _____

- What is the English for **cavolo**? _____

- What is the English for **carota**? _____

- What is the English for **aglio**? _____

- What is the English for **pisello**? _____

- What is the English for **bistecca**? _____

- What is the English for **agnello**? _____

- What is the English for **carne**? _____

- What is the English for **minestra**? _____

← *Look back for the answers*

☐ *You can write your answers in*

- What is the Italian for **mushroom**? ———————————

- What is the Italian for **onion**? ———————————

- What is the Italian for **cabbage**? ———————————

- What is the Italian for **carrot**? ———————————

- What is the Italian for **garlic**? ———————————

- What is the Italian for **pea**? ———————————

- What is the Italian for **steak**? ———————————

- What is the Italian for **lamb**? ———————————

- What is the Italian for **meat**? ———————————

- What is the Italian for **soup**? ———————————

← *Look back for the answers*

MORE FOODS

☐ **Think of each image in your mind's eye for about ten seconds**

- The Italian for **eggs** is (le) **uova.**　　　(WOVA)
  Imagine you **wove a** cloth with pictures of eggs
  on it.

- The Italian for **omelette** is **frittata.**　　　(FREETTATA)
  Imagine telling someone, "If this omelette is
  free—ta! ta! I'm off. It can't be any good."

- The Italian for **tomato** is **pomodoro.**　　　(POMODORO)
  Imagine a sea **commodore** eating tomatoes on
  the deck on a ship.

- The Italian for **potato** is **patata.**　　　(PATATA)
  Imagine eating spaghetti and mashed **potatoes.**

- The Italian for **veal** is **vitello.**　　　(VEETELLO)
  Imagine a German saying, "**Ve tell you** to eat
  veal in this restaurant."

- The Italian for **cake** is **torta.**　　　(TORTA)
  Imagine all the cakes in Italy are **tarts.**

- The Italian for **apple** is **mela.**　　　(MAYLA)
  Imagine someone who **mails you** apples.

- The Italian for **pear** is **pera.**　　　(PAYRA)
  Imagine a **pair a** pears.

- The Italian for **melon** is **melone.**　　　(MAYLONAY)
  Imagine **melon** stuffed with spaghetti.

- The Italian for **lemonade** is **limonata.**　　　(LEEMONATA)
  Imagine pouring a bottle of **lemonade** over your
  spaghetti.

☐ *You can write your answers in*

- What is the English for **limonata**?   _____

- What is the English for **melone**?   _____

- What is the English for **pera**?   _____

- What is the English for **mela**?   _____

- What is the English for **torta**?   _____

- What is the English for **vitello**?   _____

- What is the English for **patata**?   _____

- What is the English for **pomodoro**?   _____

- What is the English for **frittata**?   _____

- What is the English for **uova**?   _____

← *Look back for the answers*

- What is the Italian for **lemonade**? _____

- What is the Italian for **melon**? _____

- What is the Italian for **pear**? _____

- What is the Italian for **apple**? _____

- What is the Italian for **cake**? _____

- What is the Italian for **veal**? _____

- What is the Italian for **potato**? _____

- What is the Italian for **tomato**? _____

- What is the Italian for **omelette**? _____

- What is the Italian for **eggs**? _____

← *Look back for the answers*

ELEMENTARY GRAMMAR

As we learned in the last section, the word for *are* is *sono*.
The word for

- *(they) eat*   is *mangiano*
- *(they) want* is *vogliono*
- *(they) have* is *hanno*
- *(they) see*   is *vedono*

Notice that they all end in *no*.

➡ *So,*

- *They eat the veal*   is *Mangiano il vitello*
- *The dogs eat the veal*   is *I cani mangiano il vitello*
- *The sons want the mother* is *I figli vogliono la madre*
- *The cats have the carrots* is *I gatti hanno le carote*
- *The girls see the waiter*   is *Le ragazze vedono il cameriere*

Remember that

- *has* (e.g., he has)   is *ha*
- *wants* (e.g., he wants) is *vuole*
- *eats* (e.g., he eats)   is *mangia*
- *sees* (e.g., he sees)   is *vede*

However:

- *I have* is *ho*
- *I want* is *voglio*
- *I eat*   is *mangio*
- *I see*   is *vedo*

They all end in *o*.

➡ *So,*

- *I eat a cow*   is *Mangio una mucca*
- *I see a lamb* is *Vedo un agnello*

Note that you do not normally say *I* in Italian.
The word *ho* means *I have*, the word *vedo* means *I see*, etc.
Similarly, *ha* means *he*, *she*, or *it has*, etc.

□ *(You can write your answers in)*

1. The black rats eat the yellow apples and the red carrots.

2. The husband and the wife have two daughters.

3. I see the water.

4. The beds and the drawers are empty.

5. The brothers want more wine.

_____

_____

_____

_____

_____

_____

_____

_____

□ *The answers are:*

1. I topi neri mangiano le mele gialle e le carote rosse.

2. Il marito e la moglie hanno due figlie.

3. Vedo l'acqua.

4. I letti e i cassetti sono vuoti.

5. I fratelli vogliono più vino.

☐ **Now cover up the answers below and translate the following:**

☐ *(You can write your answers in)*

1. Il marito e la moglie mangiano due agnelli neri e l'aglio.

2. Due frittate sono sempre piccole, ma la minestra non è cara.

3. Presto le carote e le patate sono nere.

4. La sorella e il fratello vogliono sette torte adesso.

5. I letti sono piccoli.

_____

_____

_____

_____

_____

_____

_____

☐ *The answers are:*

1. The husband and the wife eat two black lambs and the garlic.

2. Two omelettes are always small, but the soup is not expensive.

3. Soon the carrots and the potatoes are black.

4. The sister and the brother want seven cakes now.

5. The beds are small.

SOME MORE USEFUL WORDS

☐ **Think of each image in your mind's eye for about ten seconds**

- The Italian for **on** is **su.** (SOO)
  Imagine someone **sues** you *on* the slightest
  pretext.

- The Italian for **in** is **in.** (EEN)
  Imagine being covered **in** spaghetti.

- The Italian for **at** and **to** is **a.** (A)
  Imagine saying, "**Ah,** I know what he's *at,* but
  I don't know what *to* do."

- The Italian for **of** is **di.** (DEE)
  Imagine the *d of* **Dundee.**

- The Italian for **from** is **da.** (DA)
  Imagine a baby getting a hug *from* **da da.**

☐ *You can write your answers in*

- What is the English for **da**?   _____

- What is the English for **di**?   _____

- What is the English for **a**?   _____

- What is the English for **in**?   _____

- What is the English for **su**?   _____

← *Look back for the answers*

☐ *You can write your answers in*

- What is the Italian for **from**? _____

- What is the Italian for **of**? _____

- What is the Italian for **at** or **to**? _____

- What is the Italian for **in**? _____

- What is the Italian for **on**? _____

← *Look back for the answers*

☐ **Now cover up the answers below and translate the following:**

☐ *(You can write your answers in)*

1. The dog is on a chair, but the cat is on a table.

2. The butter is in a cupboard, and the bread is in a drawer.

3. The soup and the meat are from a restaurant.

4. The husband sees the wife at a restaurant.

5. The sister wants a plate of peas and a glass of white wine.

_____

_____

_____

_____

_____

_____

_____

_____

☐ *The answers are:*

1. Il cane è su una sedia, ma il gatto è su una tavola.

2. Il burro è in un armadio, e il pane è in un cassetto.

3. La minestra e la carne sono da un ristorante.

4. Il marito vede la moglie a un ristorante.

5. La sorella vuole un piatto di piselli e un bicchiere di vino bianco.

☐ **Now cover up the answers below and translate the following:**

☐ *(You can write your answers in)*

1. La bistecca è su una tavola gialla.

2. Le anitre mangiano le uova dure in una stanza.

3. Ho un piatto di cipolle e un piatto di pomodori.

4. Il cameriere ha un fungo da un ristorante e un cavolo da un giardino.

5. Le pere e la limonata sono su una sedia o su un tappeto, ma il melone e il vitello sono in un cassetto.

_____

_____

_____

_____

_____

_____

☐ *The answers are:*

1. The steak is on a yellow table.

2. The ducks eat the hard eggs in a room.

3. I have a plate of onions and a plate of tomatoes.

4. The waiter has a mushroom from a restaurant and a cabbage from a garden.

5. The pears and the lemonade are on a chair or on a carpet, but the melon and the veal are in a drawer.

SECTION 7

SHOPPING AND BUSINESS WORDS

BUSINESS WORDS

☐ **Think of each image in your mind's eye for about ten seconds**

- The Italian for **owner** is **proprietario.** (PROPREEAYTAREEO)
  Imagine asking to see the **proprietor,**
  the owner of the business.

- The Italian for **manager** is **direttore.** (DEERETTORAY)
  Imagine asking to see the manager, and the
  board of **directors** is brought to see you.

- The Italian for **boss** is **padrone.** (PADRONAY)
  Imagine the boss of a firm **patronized** by
  everyone.

- The Italian for **work** is **lavoro.** (LAVORO)
  Imagine being told to **love or** work, but not
  both.

- The Italian for **factory** is **fabbrica.** (FABBREEKA)
  Imagine a factory making **fabrics.**

- The Italian for **salary** or **wage** is **salario.** (SALAREEO)
  Imagine spending your **salary** on spaghetti.

- The Italian for **product** is **prodotto.** (PRODOTTO)
  Imagine a factory whose sole **product** is
  spaghetti.

- The Italian for **firm** (company) is **ditta.** (DEETTA)
  Imagine making a **detour** to look over a firm.

- The Italian for **check** is **assegno.** (ASSENYO)
  Imagine **I send you** a check.

- The Italian for **office** is **ufficio.** (OOFEECHO)
  Imagine telling someone in your office,
  "Your feet show."

☐ *You can write your answers in*

- What is the English for **ufficio**?   _____

- What is the English for **assegno**?   _____

- What is the English for **ditta**?   _____

- What is the English for **prodotto**?   _____

- What is the English for **salario**?   _____

- What is the English for **fabbrica**?   _____

- What is the English for **lavoro**?   _____

- What is the English for **padrone**?   _____

- What is the English for **direttore**?   _____

- What is the English for **proprietario**?   _____

← *Look back for the answers*

☐ *You can write your answers in*

- What is the Italian for **office**? _____

- What is the Italian for **check**? _____

- What is the Italian for **firm**? _____

- What is the Italian for **product**? _____

- What is the Italian for **salary/wage**? _____

- What is the Italian for **factory**? _____

- What is the Italian for **work**? _____

- What is the Italian for **boss**? _____

- What is the Italian for **manager**? _____

- What is the Italian for **owner**? _____

← *Look back for the answers*

ELEMENTARY GRAMMAR

As we saw in the last section, there is no problem about any prepositions with the word *a*.

➜ *For example,*

- *on a cat* is *su un gatto*

However, when you use the word *the*, for example, *on the cat*, then things get a bit more complicated.

What you do is join the word for *on* to the word for *the*.

For example, join *su* and *il* so that *on the* becomes *sul*.

Therefore, *on the cat* becomes *sul gatto* (**not** *su il gatto*).

Similarly *at the* becomes *al*, so that *at the drawer* becomes *al cassetto* (**not** *a il cassetto*), and so on.

For feminine nouns, you also run the words *on* and *the* (*la*) together:

- *on the table*   becomes *sulla tavola*
- *at the table*   is   *alla tavola*
- *from the table* is   *dalla tavola*

☐ **Now cover up the answers below and translate the following:**

☐ *(You can write your answers in)*

1. The dog eats from the floor.

2. The manager is on the carpet.

3. The boss is at the factory.

4. The product is at the door.

5. The check is from the mother.

_____

_____

_____

_____

_____

_____

_____

_____

☐ *The answers are:*

1. Il cane mangia dal pavimento.

2. Il direttore è sul tappeto.

3. Il padrone è alla fabbrica.

4. Il prodotto è alla porta.

5. L'assegno è dalla madre.

☐ **Now cover up the answers below and translate the following:**

☐ *(You can write your answers in)*

1. Il proprietario è sulla tavola.

2. Il salario è molto piccolo.

3. Il proprietario e il direttore sono al ristorante.

4. Gli assegni sono sempre sporchi.

5. Il ragazzo è alla ditta.

_____

_____

_____

_____

_____

_____

_____

_____

☐ *The answers are:*

1. The owner is on the table.
2. The salary is very small.
3. The owner and the manager are at the restaurant.
4. The checks are always dirty.
5. The boy is at the company.

MORE BUSINESS WORDS

☐ **Think of each image in your mind's eye for about ten seconds**

- The Italian for **goods** is (la) **merce.** (MAIRCHAY)
  Imagine goods and **merchandise.**

- The Italian for **vacation** is (le) **vacanze.** (VAKANTSAY)
  Imagine there is a **vacancy** in the vacation
  hotel.

- The Italian for **price** is **prezzo.** (PRETSO)
  Imagine asking the price of a **pretzel.**

- The Italian for **mistake** is **errore.** (ERRORAY)
  Imagine your work being full of mistakes and
  errors.

- The Italian for **market** is **mercato.** (MAIRKATO)
  Imagine a **market** where all they sell is
  spaghetti.

- The Italian for **shop** is **negozio.** (NAYGOTSEEO)
  Imagine **negotiating** the price of goods in a
  shop.

- The Italian for **store clerk** is **commessa.** (KOMMESSA)
  Imagine a store clerk saying, "**Come here, sir,**
  and try this on."

- The Italian for **cashier** (cash register) is **cassa.** (KASSA)
  Imagine handing over your **cash here** to the cashier.

- The Italian for **secretary** is **segretaria.** (SEGRETAREEA)
  Imagine your **secretary** all covered in spaghetti.

- The Italian for **worker** is **operaio.** (OPER Y O)*
  Imagine an **operative** worker in a factory.

*Note: In this pronunciation, the Y is as in the English *my.*

☐ *You can write your answers in*

- What is the English for **operaio**?   _____

- What is the English for **segretaria**?   _____

- What is the English for **cassa**?   _____

- What is the English for **commessa**?   _____

- What is the English for **negozio**?   _____

- What is the English for **mercato**?   _____

- What is the English for **errore**?   _____

- What is the English for **prezzo**?   _____

- What is the English for **vacanze**?   _____

- What is the English for **merce**?   _____

← *Look back for the answers*

- What is the Italian for **worker**?　　　　　———————

- What is the Italian for **secretary**?　　　———————

- What is the Italian for **cashier**?　　　　———————

- What is the Italian for **store clerk**?　　———————

- What is the Italian for **shop**?　　　　　———————

- What is the Italian for **market**?　　　　———————

- What is the Italian for **mistake**?　　　　———————

- What is the Italian for **price**?　　　　　———————

- What is the Italian for **vacation**?　　　———————

- What is the Italian for **goods**?　　　　　———————

← *Look back for the answers*

ELEMENTARY GRAMMAR

Words like *in* and *of* also change when they are used with the word *the*.

In and *The*

You will remember that *in a drawer* is *in un cassetto*.

→ *However,*

- *in the drawer* becomes *nel cassetto*

  (Imagine Little *Nell* in the drawer)

For feminine nouns, *nel* becomes *nella*.

→ *So,*

- *in the room* becomes *nella stanza*

Of and *The*

Similarly the word *of* becomes *del* when used with *the*.

→ *So,*

- *of the dog* becomes *del cane*

  (Imagine thinking of the *dell*)

For feminine nouns *del* becomes *della*

→ *So,*

- *of the onion* becomes *della cipolla*

☐ **Now cover up the answers below and translate the following:**

☐ *(You can write your answers in)*

1. The cash register is in the shop.

2. The secretary of the company is in the room.

3. The price of the hat is high.

4. The check is in the jacket.

5. The worker is in the factory.

_____

_____

_____

_____

_____

_____

_____

_____

☐ *The answers are:*

1. La cassa è nel negozio.

2. La segretaria della ditta è nella stanza.

3. Il prezzo del cappello è alto.

4. L'assegno è nella giacca.

5. L'operaio è nella fabbrica.

☐ **Now cover up the answers below and translate the following:**

☐ *(You can write your answers in)*

1. L'ufficio della ditta è nella fabbrica.

2. Ha un negozio nel mercato.

3. Il prezzo di un operaio è molto caro.

4. La commessa è alla fabbrica.

5. Le merci sono in un armadio.

☐ *The answers are:*

1. The office of the company is in the factory.

2. He (or she) has a shop in the market.

3. The price of a worker is very expensive.

4. The store clerk is at the factory.

5. The goods are in a cupboard.

TRAVELING, THE CAR

TRAVEL WORDS

☐ **Think of each image in your mind's eye for about ten seconds**

- The Italian for **passport** is **passaporto.** (PASSAPORTO)
  Imagine spilling spaghetti all over your
  passport.

- The Italian for **customs** is **dogana.** (DOGANA)
  Imagine declaring a **dog and a** cat to customs.

- The Italian for **currency exchange** is **cambio.** (KAMBYO)
  Imagine you **can buy** money at the currency exchange.

- The Italian for **money** is **denaro.** (DENARO)
  Imagine buying **dinner** with your money.

- The Italian for **ticket** is **biglietto.** (BEELYETTO)
  Imagine someone asking if you have had the
  bill yet for your tickets.

- The Italian for **toilet** is **gabinetto.** (GABEENETTO)
  Imagine a kitchen **cabinet** being next to a toilet.

- The Italian for **entrance** is **entrata.** (ENTRATA)
  Imagine the **entrance to** your hotel all covered
  with spaghetti.

- The Italian for **exit** is **uscita.** (OOSHEETA)
  Imagine someone shouting **"You cheater"**
  as you run for the exit.

- The Italian for **station** is (la) **stazione.** (STATSYONAY)
  Imagine a **station** platform all covered in
  spaghetti.

- The Italian for **danger** is **pericolo.** (PAYREEKOLO)
  Imagine the famous singer **Perry Como**
  shouting to you—"Danger! Danger!"

- What is the English for **pericolo**? _____

- What is the English for **stazione**? _____

- What is the English for **uscita**? _____

- What is the English for **entrata**? _____

- What is the English for **gabinetto**? _____

- What is the English for **biglietto**? _____

- What is the English for **denaro**? _____

- What is the English for **cambio**? _____

- What is the English for **dogana**? _____

- What is the English for **passaporto**? _____

← *Look back for the answers*

☐ *You can write your answers in*

- What is the Italian for **danger**?   _____

- What is the Italian for **station**?   _____

- What is the Italian for **exit**?   _____

- What is the Italian for **entrance**?   _____

- What is the Italian for **toilet**?   _____

- What is the Italian for **ticket**?   _____

- What is the Italian for **money**?   _____

- What is the Italian for **currency
  exchange**?   _____

- What is the Italian for **customs**?   _____

- What is the Italian for **passport**?   _____

← *Look back for the answers*

ELEMENTARY GRAMMAR

The Italian for *am,* for example in *I am a father,* is *sono.*

➜ *So,*

- *I am a father* is *Sono un padre*

Please note that the word *I* is normally left out in Italian. In fact, all personal pronouns like *I, he she, it,* etc., are nearly always left out (but you need not worry about the exceptions).

➜ *So,*

- *She is a mother* is *È una madre*

- *It is a ticket* is *È un biglietto*

Remember that when you say something like *I am tired,* the sentence in Italian is either *Sono stanco* or *Sono stanca* depending on whether the speaker is male or female.

Also, when you say something like *It is dirty,* then the gender of whatever *it* refers to will affect the ending of the adjective.

For example, if *it* is a table, then

- *It is dirty* is *È sporca* (because *tavola* is feminine)

If *it* is a dog, then

- *It is dirty* is *È sporco* (because *cane* is masculine)

☐ **Now cover up the answers below and translate the following:**

☐ *(You can write your answers in)*

1. I am always tired.

2. It is a dirty passport.

3. He has money and a ticket.

4. She wants the toilet.

5. It is the exit from the station.

_____

_____

_____

_____

_____

_____

_____

☐ *The answers are:*

1. Sono sempre stanco (or stanca).

2. È un passaporto sporco.

3. Ha denaro e un biglietto.

4. Vuole il gabinetto.
   (You can also use the word *toilette*—pronounced TWALET.)

5. È l'uscita dalla stazione.

SOME MORE TRAVEL WORDS

☐ **Think of each image in your mind's eye for about ten seconds**

- The Italian for **boat** is **battello.** (BATTELLO)
  Imagine sailing into **battle** on a boat.

- The Italian for **train** is **treno.** (TRAYNO)
  Imagine a **train** with spaghetti trailing from
  every window.

- The Italian for **car** is **macchina.** (MAKKEENA)
  Imagine your car as a shiny new **machine.**

- The Italian for **street** is **strada.** (STRADA)
  Imagine a group of people **straddling** the street.

- The Italian for **bridge** is **ponte.** (PONTAY)
  Imagine a group of people all **point to** a
  bridge.

- The Italian for **map** is **mappa.** (MAPPA)
  Imagine a **map** all covered in little bits of
  spaghetti.

- The Italian for **gasoline** is **benzina.** (BENTSEENA)
  Imagine a sign at a gasoline station "**Benzine**
  for sale."

- The Italian for **oil** is **olio.** (OLYO)
  Imagine someone threatening to **oil you** by
  pouring a can of oil over your head.

- The Italian for **garage** is **garage.** (GARAJ)
  Imagine a **garage** floor all covered in spaghetti.

- The Italian for **traffic lights** is **semaforo.** (SAYMAFORO)
  Imagine that the traffic lights have broken down
  and a police officer is using **semaphore** flags
  instead to direct traffic.

□ *You can write your answers in*

- What is the English for **semaforo**? _____

- What is the English for **garage**? _____

- What is the English for **olio**? _____

- What is the English for **benzina**? _____

- What is the English for **mappa**? _____

- What is the English for **ponte**? _____

- What is the English for **strada**? _____

- What is the English for **macchina**? _____

- What is the English for **treno**? _____

- What is the English for **battello**? _____

← *Look back for the answers*

☐ *You can write your answers in*

- What is the Italian for **traffic lights**?   _____

- What is the Italian for **garage**?   _____

- What is the Italian for **oil**?   _____

- What is the Italian for **gasoline**?   _____

- What is the Italian for **map**?   _____

- What is the Italian for **bridge**?   _____

- What is the Italian for **street**?   _____

- What is the Italian for **car**?   _____

- What is the Italian for **train**?   _____

- What is the Italian for **boat**?   _____

← *Look back for the answers*

SOME MORE USEFUL WORDS

☐ **Think of each image in your mind's eye for about ten seconds**

- The Italian for **here** is **qui.** (KWEE)
  Imagine being told that the **quee**n is *here*.

- The Italian for **there** is **lì.** (LEE)
  Imagine thinking "*There* is the **lee**k."

- The Italian for **first** is **primo.** (PREEMO)
  Imagine having a **premonition** that you will be *first* in your class.

- The Italian for **last** is **ultimo.** (OOLTEEMO)
  Imagine giving an **ultimatum**—a *last* warning.

- The Italian for **second** is **secondo.** (SAYKONDO)
  Imagine asking for a **second** helping of spaghetti.

☐ *You can write your answers in*

- What is the English for **secondo**? _____

- What is the English for **ultimo**? _____

- What is the English for **primo**? _____

- What is the English for **lì**? _____

- What is the English for **qui**? _____

← *Look back for the answers*

☐ *You can write your answers in*

- What is the Italian for **second**? _____

- What is the Italian for **last**? _____

- What is the Italian for **first**? _____

- What is the Italian for **there**? _____

- What is the Italian for **here**? _____

← *Look back for the answers*

ELEMENTARY GRAMMAR

Almost all adjectives come after the noun.

➜ *For example,*

- *gatto nero*   for *black cat*

- *marito brutto* for *ugly husband*

However, the words *primo, ultimo,* and *secondo* come before the noun.

➜ *So,*

- *It is the first boat* is *È il primo battello*

- *It is the last train* is *È l'ultimo treno*

☐ **Now cover up the answers below and translate the following:**

☐ *(You can write your answers in)*

1. The first boat is here.

2. The last train is in the station.

3. The street is here.

4. The second bridge is there.

5. The entrance is there.

_____

_____

_____

_____

_____

_____

_____

☐ *The answers are:*

1. Il primo battello è qui.

2. L'ultimo treno è nella stazione.

3. La strada è qui.

4. Il secondo ponte è lì.

5. L'entrata è lì.

☐ **Now cover up the answers below and translate the following:**

☐ *(You can write your answers in)*

1. La macchina è pesante e nera.

2. Il cambio è lì, ma è caro.

3. Pericolo! La dogana è qui.

4. I semafori sono sempre rossi qui.

5. Il garage ha la mappa e l'olio.

_____

_____

_____

_____

_____

_____

_____

☐ *The answers are:*

1. The car is heavy and black.
2. The currency exchange is there, but it is expensive.
3. Danger! The customs is here.
4. The traffic lights are always red here.
5. The garage has the map and the oil.

MORE TRAVELING WORDS

☐ **Think of each image in your mind's eye for about ten seconds**

- The Italian for **breakdown** is **guasto.**   (GWASTO)
  Imagine telling the garage that something
  ghastly has happened, your car has broken
  down.

- The Italian for **driver** is **autista.**   (OWTEESTA)
  Imagine an **artist** driving a car, with an easel
  and paint in the back.

- The Italian for **brake** is **freno.**   (FRAYNO)
  Imagine being told "Don't be **afraid.** The
  brakes do work."

- The Italian for **spark plug** is **candela.**   (KANDAYLA)
  Imagine using **candles** instead of spark plugs,
  in your car.

- The Italian for **hood** is **cofano.**   (KOFANO)
  Imagine a **coffin** being placed on the hood of
  your car.

- The Italian for **battery** is **batteria.**   (BATTAIREEA)
  Imagine a **battery** covered in spaghetti.

- The Italian for **wheel** is **ruota.**   (RWOTA)
  Imagine a wheel on the end of your **rotor**
  blades.

- The Italian for **tire** is **gomma.**   (GOMMA)
  Imagine your tire made of **gummy** material and
  getting all soft.

- The Italian for **steering wheel** is **volante.**   (VOLANTAY)
  Imagine **violently** grabbing at the steering
  wheel.

- The Italian for **jack** is **cricco.**   (KREEKO)
  Imagine being up the **creek** without a jack after
  a flat tire.

- What is the English for **cricco**?   _____

- What is the English for **volante**?   _____

- What is the English for **gomma**?   _____

- What is the English for **ruota**?   _____

- What is the English for **batteria**?   _____

- What is the English for **cofano**?   _____

- What is the English for **candela**?   _____

- What is the English for **freno**?   _____

- What is the English for **autista**?   _____

- What is the English for **guasto**?   _____

← *Look back for the answers*

- What is the Italian for **jack**?   _____

- What is the Italian for **steering wheel**?   _____

- What is the Italian for **tire**?   _____

- What is the Italian for **wheel**?   _____

- What is the Italian for **battery**?   _____

- What is the Italian for **hood**?   _____

- What is the Italian for **spark plug**?   _____

- What is the Italian for **brake**?   _____

- What is the Italian for **driver**?   _____

- What is the Italian for **breakdown**?   _____

← *Look back for the answers*

SOME MORE USEFUL WORDS

☐ **Think of each image in your mind's eye for about ten seconds**

- The Italian for **where** is **dove.** (DOVAY)
  Imagine asking, "*Where* is the **dove of** peace?"

- The Italian for **why** is **perché.** (PAIRKAY)
  Imagine asking, "*Why* are you so **perky**?"

- The Italian for **which** is **quale.** (KWALAY)
  Imagine asking, "*Which* **koala** bear do you want?"

- The Italian for **how much** is **quanto.** (KWANTO)
  Imagine asking, "*How much* is the bottle of **cointreau?**"

- The Italian for **who** is **chi.** (KEE)
  Imagine wondering *who* has got your **key.**

□ *You can write your answers in*

- What is the English for **chi**? _____

- What is the English for **quanto**? _____

- What is the English for **quale**? _____

- What is the English for **perché**? _____

- What is the English for **dove**? _____

← *Look back for the answers*

☐ *You can write your answers in*

- What is the Italian for **who**? _____

- What is the Italian for **how much**? _____

- What is the Italian for **which**? _____

- What is the Italian for **why**? _____

- What is the Italian for **where**? _____

← *Look back for the answers*

ELEMENTARY GRAMMAR

Please note that when the word *dove* (where) is used with the word *is*, for example, *Where is the dog?*, then *where is* becomes *dov'è* with the stress on the *è*.

➜ *So,*

   • *Where is the dog?* is *Dov'è il cane?*

☐ **Now cover up the answers below and translate the following:**

☐ *(You can write your answers in)*

1. Where is the passport?—It is here.

2. Who is the girl?

3. Why am I here?

4. How much is the gasoline?

5. Which horse is first?

_____

_____

_____

_____

_____

_____

_____

☐ *The answers are:*

1. Dov'è il passaporto?—È qui.

2. Chi è la ragazza?

3. Perché sono qui?

4. Quanto è la benzina?

5. Quale cavallo è primo?

☐ **Now cover up the answers below and translate the following:**

☐ *(You can write your answers in)*

1. La macchina è pesante e nera, e il guasto è cattivo.

2. Dov'è la batteria, e dov'è la gomma?

3. Il freno, perché è sporco, e la candela, perché è verde?

4. Chi è l'autista, e dov'è il cricco?

5. Il cofano e la ruota sono molto duri, ma il volante perché non è pulito?

_____

_____

_____

_____

_____

_____

☐ *The answers are:*

1. The car is heavy and black, and the breakdown is bad.

2. Where is the battery, and where is the tire?

3. Why is the brake dirty and why is the spark plug green?

4. Who is the driver, and where is the jack?

5. The hood and the wheel are very hard, but why is the steering wheel not clean?

Notice that in a question involving the word *why* (*perché*), the subject of the question is often placed first, with *perché* and the verb following.

SECTION 9

LEISURE ACTIVITIES

ON THE BEACH

☐ **Think of each image in your mind's eye for about ten seconds**

- The Italian for **sea** is **mare.** (MARAY)
  Imagine you watch a couple **marry** in the sea.

- The Italian for **bay** is **baia.** (BY YA)
  Imagine a rich man boasting "I'll **buy you** this bay."

- The Italian for **sand** is **sabbia.** (SABBYA)
  Imagine that sand **saps your** strength when you walk on it.

- The Italian for **sun** is **sole.** (SOLAY)
  Imagine the sun shining **so you lay** on the beach.

- The Italian for **hot** is **caldo.** (KALDO)
  Imagine **cold** water comes out of the hot faucet.

- The Italian for **cold** is **freddo.** (FREDDO)
  Imagine being **afraid o'** the cold.

- The Italian for **bucket** is **secchia.** (SEKKYA)
  Imagine that for safety's **sake, you** put your bucket under the stairs.

- The Italian for **picnic** is **picnic.** (PEEKNEEK)
  Imagine you have cold spaghetti for your **picnic.**

- The Italian for **help** is **aiuto.** (AYOOTO)
  Imagine shouting, "**Ah! You two** help me!"

- The Italian for **game** is **gioco.** (JOKO)
  Imagine the game you are playing is a bit of a **joke.**

☐ *You can write your answers in*

- What is the English for **gioco**? _____

- What is the English for **aiuto**? _____

- What is the English for **picnic**? _____

- What is the English for **secchia**? _____

- What is the English for **freddo**? _____

- What is the English for **caldo**? _____

- What is the English for **sole**? _____

- What is the English for **sabbia**? _____

- What is the English for **baia**? _____

- What is the English for **mare**? _____

← *Look back for the answers*

- What is the Italian for **game**? _____

- What is the Italian for **help**? _____

- What is the Italian for **picnic**? _____

- What is the Italian for **bucket**? _____

- What is the Italian for **cold**? _____

- What is the Italian for **hot**? _____

- What is the Italian for **sun**? _____

- What is the Italian for **sand**? _____

- What is the Italian for **bay**? _____

- What is the Italian for **sea**? _____

← *Look back for the answers*

MORE LEISURE WORDS

☐ **Think of each image in your mind's eye for about ten seconds**

- The Italian for **countryside** is **campagna.** (KAMPANYA)
  Imagine going with a **companion** into the
  countryside.

- The Italian for **river** is **fiume.** (FYOOMAY)
  Imagine a river going so fast that **few may** get
  across.

- The Italian for **mountain** is **montagna.** (MONTANYA)
  Imagine the state of **Montana,** with high
  mountains.

- The Italian for **lake** is **lago.** (LAGO)
  Imagine a lake filled with **lager** beer.

- The Italian for **newspaper** is **giornale.** (JORNALAY)
  Imagine a **journal** made up of old newspapers.

- The Italian for **book** is **libro.** (LEEBRO)
  Imagine a **library** full of books.

- The Italian for **letter** is **lettera.** (LETTERA)
  Imagine a **letter** all covered in spaghetti.

- The Italian for **stamp** is **francobollo.** (FRANKOBOLLO)
  Imagine having some French **francs in
  a bowl** when you go to buy stamps.

- The Italian for **envelope** is **busta.** (BOOSTA)
  Imagine you **bust a** envelope open when you
  are buying a package of them.

- The Italian for **excursion** is **gita.** (JEETA)
  Imagine saying, "**Gee ta!**" when someone
  offers to take you on an exciting excursion.

- What is the English for **gita**? ⸻

- What is the English for **busta**? ⸻

- What is the English for **francobollo**? ⸻

- What is the English for **lettera**? ⸻

- What is the English for **libro**? ⸻

- What is the English for **giornale**? ⸻

- What is the English for **lago**? ⸻

- What is the English for **montagna**? ⸻

- What is the English for **fiume**? ⸻

- What is the English for **campagna**? ⸻

← *Look back for the answers*

☐ *You can write your answers in*

- What is the Italian for **excursion**? _____

- What is the Italian for **envelope**? _____

- What is the Italian for **stamp**? _____

- What is the Italian for **letter**? _____

- What is the Italian for **book**? _____

- What is the Italian for **newspaper**? _____

- What is the Italian for **lake**? _____

- What is the Italian for **mountain**? _____

- What is the Italian for **river**? _____

- What is the Italian for **countryside**? _____

← *Look back for the answers*

ELEMENTARY GRAMMAR

You will remember that the Italian for *I am* is *sono*.

In Italian, the word for:

- *I eat*   is *mangio*

- *I have* is *ho*

- *I want* is *voglio*

- *I see*   is *vedo*

In other words, all of these verbs end in an *o* when you say *I want, I see,* etc.

Please note that you use the same word if you want to say *I am eating,* etc. Remember, *I* always ends in *o*.

➜ *For example,*

- *I see a dog*   is *Vedo un cane*

- *I want a passport*   is *Voglio un passaporto*

- *I am eating a duck* is *Mangio un'anitra*

- *I have a bucket*   is *Ho una secchia*

Please note, also, that *mangia* for *eats* can also be used to say *he is eating*.

Similarly, *vede* can mean *he* or *she is seeing* as well as *he* or *she sees,* and so on for all verbs.

☐ **Now cover up the answers below and translate the following:**

☐ *(You can write your answers in)*

1. I see the blue sea and the golden sand.

2. I want the game here, not there.

3. The sun is very hot, but the river is cold.

4. I am eating a picnic on the lake.

5. I have a newspaper and an expensive book.

_____

_____

_____

_____

_____

_____

_____

☐ *The answers are:*

1. Vedo il mare blu e la sabbia d'oro.

2. Voglio il gioco qui, non lì.

3. Il sole è molto caldo, ma il fiume è freddo.

4. Mangio un picnic sul lago.

5. Ho un giornale e un libro caro.

☐ **Now cover up the answers below and translate the following:**

☐ *(You can write your answers in)*

1. Il cane vuole la secchia pesante, e vuole le lettere rosse.

2. La gita è molto tranquilla e il picnic è cattivo.

3. Giorgio ha un libro sporco e vede una baia sporca.

4. Aiuto! Vedo la montagna fredda e la campagna marrone.

5. Voglio il sole caldo e voglio il mare freddo.

_____

_____

_____

_____

_____

_____

_____

_____

☐ *The answers are:*

1. The dog wants the heavy bucket and he wants the red letters.
2. The excursion is very quiet and the picnic is bad.
3. Giorgio has a dirty book and he sees a dirty bay.
4. Help! I see the cold mountain and the brown countryside.
5. I want the hot sun and I want the cold sea.

SOME MORE USEFUL WORDS

☐ **Think of each image in your mind's eye for about ten seconds**

- The Italian for **I drink** is **bevo.**   (BAYVO)
  Imagine *drinking* a **beverage.**

- The Italian for **I put** is **metto.**   (METTO)
  Imagine I *put* **metal** on a table.

- The Italian for **I speak** is **parlo.**   (PARLO)
  Imagine people *speaking* in the **parlor.**

- The Italian for **I sell** is **vendo.**   (VENDO)
  Imagine a street **vendor** *selling* you something.

Note that you use the same words for *I am drinking, I am going,* etc.

☐ *You can write your answers in*

- What is the English for **vendo**?   _____

- What is the English for **parlo**?   _____

- What is the English for **metto**?   _____

- What is the English for **bevo**?   _____

← *Look back for the answers*

☐ *You can write your answers in*

- What is the Italian for **I sell**? _____

- What is the Italian for **I speak**? _____

- What is the Italian for **I put**? _____

- What is the Italian for **I drink**? _____

← *Look back for the answers*

GENERALLY USEFUL WORDS

☐ **Think of each image in your mind's eye for about ten seconds**

- The Italian for **doctor** is **dottore.** (DOTTORAY)
  Imagine a **doddery** old doctor listening to your chest.

- The Italian for **dentist** is (il) **dentista.** (DENTEESTA)
  Imagine a **dentist** with spaghetti between her teeth.

- The Italian for **lawyer** is **avvocato.** (AVVOKATO)
  Imagine a lawyer eating an **avocado.**

- The Italian for **police officer** is **poliziotto.** (POLEETSYOTTO)
  Imagine a police officer standing on a **police yacht oh!**

- The Italian for **bank** is **banca.** (BANKA)
  Imagine depositing spaghetti in a **bank.**

- The Italian for **hotel** is **albergo.** (ALBAIRGO)
  Imagine you see a sign saying "**All bears go** to this hotel."
  (Remember the word for *tree* is *albero.*)

- The Italian for **hospital** is **ospedale.** (OSPAYDALAY)
  Imagine they give you nothing but spaghetti in the **hospital.**

- The Italian for **church** is **chiesa.** (KYAYZA)
  Imagine you have the **keys of a** church.

- The Italian for **museum** is **museo.** (MOOZAYO)
  Imagine an exhibition of spaghetti in a **museum.**

- The Italian for **castle** is **castello.** (KASTELLO)
  Imagine Lou **Costello** of Abbott and Costello, looking over the parapet of a castle.

- What is the English for **castello**? ——————

- What is the English for **museo**? ——————

- What is the English for **chiesa**? ——————

- What is the English for **ospedale**? ——————

- What is the English for **albergo**? ——————

- What is the English for **banca**? ——————

- What is the English for **poliziotto**? ——————

- What is the English for **avvocato**? ——————

- What is the English for **dentista**? ——————

- What is the English for **dottore**? ——————

← *Look back for the answers*

☐ *You can write your answers in*

- What is the Italian for **castle**? _____

- What is the Italian for **museum**? _____

- What is the Italian for **church**? _____

- What is the Italian for **hospital**? _____

- What is the Italian for **hotel**? _____

- What is the Italian for **bank**? _____

- What is the Italian for **police officer**? _____

- What is the Italian for **lawyer**? _____

- What is the Italian for **dentist**? _____

- What is the Italian for **doctor**? _____

← *Look back for the answers*

☐ **Now cover up the answers below and translate the following:**

☐ *(You can write your answers in)*

1. I am drinking a glass of hot milk.

2. I am at the church.

3. I am putting a stamp on the envelope.

4. I am speaking to the doctor, but not to the lawyer.

5. I am selling a hotel and a castle.

_____

_____

_____

_____

_____

_____

☐ *The answers are:*

1. Bevo un bicchiere di latte caldo.

2. Sono alla chiesa.

3. Metto un francobollo sulla busta.

4. Parlo al dottore, ma non all'avvocato.

5. Vendo un albergo e un castello.

Please note: When the noun begins with a vowel, for example in *avvocato,* then *al* or *alla* becomes *all'. Al* and *all'* sound very similar.

198

Now cover up the answers below and translate the following:

☐ *(You can write your answers in)*

1. Vendo la sabbia calda.

2. Aiuto! Metto la lettera sulla tavola.

3. Vendo il francobollo.

4. Parlo al marito.

5. Bevo il vino.

_____

_____

_____

_____

_____

_____

_____

_____

☐ *The answers are:*

1. I am selling the hot sand.
2. Help! I am putting the letter on the table.
3. I am selling the stamp.
4. I am speaking to the husband.
5. I am drinking the wine.

ELEMENTARY GRAMMAR

You will remember from an earlier section that when you want to say *they eat, they want,* etc., then the word ends in *no.*

→ *So,*

- *they want* is *vogliono*

- *they eat* is *mangiano*

- *they have* is *hanno*

- *they see* is *vedono*

Similarly, the same is true of the words you learned in the last section.

→ *So,*

- *they drink* is *bevono*

- *they put* is *mettono*

- *they speak* is *parlano*

- *they sell* is *vendono*

→ *For example,*

- *They drink the tea* is *Bevono il tè*

- *They drink in a room* is *Bevono in una stanza*

- *They speak to a frog* is *Parlano a una rana*

Note:

If one says, *the boy and the girl speak, see,* etc., then the words for *speak* and *see* are *parlano* and *vedono,* etc.

☐ **Now cover up the answers below and translate the following:**

☐ *(You can write your answers in)*

1. The boy and the girl drink in the restaurant.

2. The fish and the horse speak to the bull.

3. The brother and the sister sell a heavy chair.

4. The bucket and the sand are in the room.

5. The husband and the wife put the stamp on the envelope.

_____

_____

_____

_____

_____

_____

_____

_____

☐ *The answers are:*

1. Il ragazzo e la ragazza bevono nel ristorante.

2. Il pesce e il cavallo parlano al toro.

3. Il fratello e la sorella vendono una sedia pesante.

4. La secchia e la sabbia sono nella stanza.

5. Il marito e la moglie mettono il francobollo sulla busta.

☐ **Now cover up the answers below and translate the following:**

☐ *(You can write your answers in)*

1. Aiuto! Dov'è l'ospedale? Voglio un dottore o un dentista.

2. Il poliziotto vede la banca.

3. Parlo e bevo.

4. Il museo ha quattro stanze strette.

5. Bevo il vino, mangio il pane e sono stanco.

_____

_____

_____

_____

_____

_____

_____

_____

☐ *The answers are:*

1. Help! Where is the hospital? I want a doctor or a dentist.

2. The police officer sees the bank.

3. I speak and drink.

4. The museum has four narrow rooms.

5. I drink the wine, I eat the bread, and I am tired.

ELEMENTARY GRAMMAR

You will remember that:

- *he has* is *ha*

- *he eats* is *mangia*

- *he sees* is *vede*

So, the word either ends in an *a* or an *e*.

It is exactly the same for the words you have just learned.

➔ *So,*

- *he drinks* is *beve*

- *he puts* is *mette*

- *she sells* is *vende*

- *he speaks* is *parla*

(*He, she,* and *it* are indicated by the ending *a* or *e*.)

➔ *So,*

- *He sells the cups* is *Vende le tazze*

- *She drinks the wine* is *Beve il vino*

- *She speaks to the dog* is *Parla al cane*

Remember that there is no need to say *he, she,* or *it* in Italian. The form of the verb is the same in all three cases.

Now cover up the answers below and translate the following:

☐ *(You can write your answers in)*

1. She has a flower, and she sells the plants.

2. He drinks the wine, and he speaks to the son.

3. She puts the newspaper on the table.

4. She is eating in a restaurant, and she sells the meat to the restaurant.

5. She sees the letters, and she has the books.

_____

_____

_____

_____

_____

_____

_____

☐ *The answers are:*

1. Ha un fiore, e vende le piante.

2. Beve il vino, e parla al figlio.

3. Mette il giornale sulla tavola.

4. Mangia in un ristorante, e vende la carne al ristorante.

5. Vede le lettere, e ha i libri.

☐ **Now cover up the answers below and translate the following:**

☐ *(You can write your answers in)*

1. Metto un libro sulla tavola.

2. Il bruco e la medusa bevono dal piatto.

3. Vendono coltelli, piatti, e forchette.

4. Il padre e la madre vedono i mari.

5. Il figlio beve, la figlia mangia, il fratello parla, e la madre vende la sabbia.

_____

_____

_____

_____

_____

_____

☐ *The answers are:*

1. I am putting a book on the table.

2. The caterpillar and the jellyfish drink from the plate.

3. They sell knives, plates, and forks.

4. The father and the mother see the seas.

5. The son drinks, the daughter eats, the brother speaks, and the mother sells the sand.

T THE DOCTOR'S, EMERGENCY WORDS, USEFUL WORDS

ILLNESS

☐ **Think of each image in your mind's eye for about ten seconds**

- The Italian for **foot** is **piede**.   (PYAYDAY)
  Imagine your wife putting her foot down when
  it comes to **pay day.**

- The Italian for **sick** is **malato**.   (MALATO)
  Imagine being sick with a mysterious **malady.**

- The Italian for **head** is **testa**.   (TESTA)
  Imagine a doctor who **tests a** head to see if it is
  still O.K.

- The Italian for **skin** is (la) **pelle**.   (PELLAY)
  Imagine your skin is **peeling.**

- The Italian for **heart** is **cuore**.   (KWORAY)
  Imagine throwing someone's heart into a
  quarry.

- The Italian for **back** is **dorso**.   (DORSO)
  Imagine the **dorsal** fin on the back of a shark.

- The Italian for **thigh** is **coscia**.   (KOSHA)
  Imagine one rabbi asking another rabbi whether
  a chicken thigh is **kosher.**

- The Italian for **stomach** is **stomaco**.   (STOMAKO)
  Imagine your **stomach** filled with spaghetti.

- The Italian for **hand** is (la) **mano**.   (MANO)
  Imagine a **man** warming his hand.

- The Italian for **leg** is **gamba**.   (GAMBA)
  Imagine **gambol**ing about on a gammy leg.

□ *You can write your answers in*

- What is the English for **gamba**? _____

- What is the English for (la) **mano**? _____

- What is the English for **stomaco**? _____

- What is the English for **coscia**? _____

- What is the English for **dorso**? _____

- What is the English for **cuore**? _____

- What is the English for (la) **pelle**? _____

- What is the English for **testa**? _____

- What is the English for **malato**? _____

- What is the English for **piede**? _____

← *Look back for the answers*

☐ *You can write your answers in*

- What is the Italian for **leg**? _____

- What is the Italian for **hand**? _____

- What is the Italian for **stomach**? _____

- What is the Italian for **thigh**? _____

- What is the Italian for **back**? _____

- What is the Italian for **heart**? _____

- What is the Italian for **skin**? _____

- What is the Italian for **head**? _____

- What is the Italian for **sick**? _____

- What is the Italian for **foot**? _____

← *Look back for the answers*

EMERGENCY AND USEFUL WORDS

☐ **Think of each image in your mind's eye for about ten seconds**

- The Italian for **bandage** is **fascia.** (FASHA)
  Imagine a **Fascist** with a bandage around his
  arm.

- The Italian for **blood** is **sangue.** (SANGWAY)
  Imagine someone who **sang away** as blood
  streamed from her head.

- The Italian for **accident** is **incidente.** (EENCHEEDENTAY)
  Imagine a nasty **incident** results in
  an accident.

- The Italian for **thief** is **ladro.** (LADRO)
  Imagine a thief with a **ladder on** his back,
  running down a street.

- The Italian for **fire** is **fuoco.** (FWOKO)
  Imagine a fire in **four courts** for playing tennis.

- The Italian for **telephone** is **telefono.** (TELAYFONO)
  Imagine a **telephone** all covered in spaghetti.

- The Italian for **ambulance** is **ambulanza.** (AMBOOLANTSA)
  Imagine loading spaghetti into an
  ambulance.

- The Italian for **lost** is **perso.** (PAIRSO)
  Imagine a **poor soul** who is lost.

- The Italian for **dead** is **morto.** (MORTO)
  Imagine people showing they are **mortal** by
  being dead.

- The Italian for **pain** is **dolore.** (DOLORAY)
  Imagine being given a **dollar** to make your pain
  go away.

- What is the English for **dolore**?　　　_____

- What is the English for **morto**?　　　_____

- What is the English for **perso**?　　　_____

- What is the English for **ambulanza**?　　_____

- What is the English for **telefono**?　　_____

- What is the English for **fuoco**?　　　_____

- What is the English for **ladro**?　　　_____

- What is the English for **incidente**?　　_____

- What is the English for **sangue**?　　　_____

- What is the English for **fascia**?　　　_____

← *Look back for the answers*

☐ *You can write your answers in*

- What is the Italian for **pain**?　　　　＿＿＿＿＿＿＿＿＿

- What is the Italian for **dead**?　　　　＿＿＿＿＿＿＿＿＿

- What is the Italian for **lost**?　　　　＿＿＿＿＿＿＿＿＿

- What is the Italian for **ambulance**?　　＿＿＿＿＿＿＿＿＿

- What is the Italian for **telephone**?　　＿＿＿＿＿＿＿＿＿

- What is the Italian for **fire**?　　　　＿＿＿＿＿＿＿＿＿

- What is the Italian for **thief**?　　　　＿＿＿＿＿＿＿＿＿

- What is the Italian for **accident**?　　　＿＿＿＿＿＿＿＿＿

- What is the Italian for **blood**?　　　　＿＿＿＿＿＿＿＿＿

- What is the Italian for **bandage**?　　　＿＿＿＿＿＿＿＿＿

← *Look back for the answers*

ELEMENTARY GRAMMAR

The word for *some* is *del*.

→ *So,*

- *some wine* is *del vino*

- *some bread* is *del pane*

This is for masculine words.

For feminine words *del* becomes *della*.

→ *So,*

- *some jam* is *della marmellata*

- *some beer* is *della birra*, etc.

→ *For example,*

- *I want some wine* is *Voglio del vino*

□ **Now cover up the answers below and translate the following:**

□ *(You can write your answers in)*

1. I want some red blood.

2. I eat some hard bread.

3. He sees some very dirty pepper.

4. She wants some very cold veal.

5. I have some yellow butter.

_____

_____

_____

_____

_____

_____

_____

_____

□ *The answers are:*

1. Voglio del sangue rosso.

2. Mangio del pane duro.

3. Vede del pepe molto sporco.

4. Vuole del vitello molto freddo.

5. Ho del burro giallo.

Now cover up the answers below and translate the following:

☐ *(You can write your answers in)*

1. Il dolore è sulla coscia e nella testa.

2. La ragazza è molto malata. Vuole un dottore.

3. Il ladro ha una mano nera, tre coltelli verdi, e sei forchette.

4. Il fuoco è molto caldo e molto rosso.

5. L'incidente è molto cattivo. La moglie è morta.

_____

_____

_____

_____

_____

_____

_____

☐ *The answers are:*

1. The pain is on the thigh and in the head.

2. The girl is very ill. She wants a doctor.

3. The thief has a black hand, three green knives, and six forks.

4. The fire is very hot and very red.

5. The accident is very bad. The wife is dead.

SOME USEFUL WORDS

☐ **Think of each image in your mind's eye for about ten seconds**

- The Italian for **please** is **per favore.** (PAIR FAVORAY)
  Imagine saying "**Pour favors,** please."

- The Italian for **thank you** is **grazie.** (GRATSEEAY)
  Imagine saying thank you **graciously.**

- The Italian for **sorry** or **excuse me** is (MEE SKOOZEE)
  mi scusi.
  Imagine saying, "Oh, **me! Excuse me** for
  stepping on your toe. Sorry!"

- The Italian for **hello** is **ciao.** (CHOW)
  Imagine saying hello to someone who throws
  chow mein at you.

- The Italian for **good night** is **buona notte.** (BWONA NOTTAY)
  Imagine putting a bad child to bed and
  saying, "Good night, you have **been a naughty**
  girl."

- The Italian for **it's a pleasure** is **prego.** (PRAYGO)
  Imagine telling someone to **pray go** and the
  person says, "It's a pleasure."

- The Italian for **how do you do** is **piacere.** (PYACHAYRAY)
  Imagine telling someone "How do you do—
  put your chair here."

- The Italian for **left** is **sinistro.** (SEENEESTRO)
  Imagine someone **sinister** who has a left arm
  covered in blood.

- The Italian for **right** is **destro.** (DESTRO)
  Imagine a Communist saying, "I will **destroy**
  all of the people on the political right."

- The Italian for **downtown** (town center) is (CHENTRO)
  centro.
  Imagine being in the **center** of traffic in the
  downtown area.

☐ *You can write your answers in*

- What is the English for **centro**?   _____

- What is the English for **destro**?   _____

- What is the English for **sinistro**?   _____

- What is the English for **piacere**?   _____

- What is the English for **prego**?   _____

- What is the English for **buona notte**?   _____

- What is the English for **ciao**?   _____

- What is the English for **mi scusi**?   _____

- What is the English for **grazie**?   _____

- What is the English for **per favore**?   _____

← *Look back for the answers*

☐ *You can write your answers in*

- What is the Italian for **downtown**? _____

- What is the Italian for **right**? _____

- What is the Italian for **left**? _____

- What is the Italian for **how do you do**? _____

- What is the Italian for **it's a pleasure**? _____

- What is the Italian for **good night**? _____

- What is the Italian for **hello**? _____

- What is the Italian for **sorry**? _____

- What is the Italian for **thank you**? _____

- What is the Italian for **please**? _____

← *Look back for the answers*

ELEMENTARY GRAMMAR

In the last section, you saw how to use the word for *some* (*del/della*).

When the noun is plural, for example, *some dogs, some chickens,* etc., then the word for *some* is *dei* (pronounced like DAY).

➜　*So,*

- *some dogs*　　is *dei cani*

- *some chickens* is *dei polli,* etc.

For feminine nouns the word for *some* is *delle*.

➜　*For example,*

- *some legs*　is *delle gambe*

- *some heads* is *delle teste,* etc.

➜　*For example,*

- *I see some legs* is *Vedo delle gambe*

☐ **Now cover up the answers below and translate the following:**

   ☐ *(You can write your answers in)*

1. The husband has a bandage, and the doctor has some blood in a cup.

2. The dog has a small foot, a dirty back, a brown leg and eats some carrots.

3. The head and the heart are very cold, but the skin and the blood are very hot.

4. "I want some telephones in the room, please"—"It's a pleasure."

5. The ambulance is lost, and downtown is empty.

_____

_____

_____

_____

_____

☐ *The answers are:*

1. Il marito ha una fascia, e il dottore ha del sangue in una tazza.

2. Il cane ha un piede piccolo, un dorso sporco, una gamba marrone e mangia delle carote.

3. La testa e il cuore sono molto freddi, ma la pelle e il sangue sono molto caldi.

4. "Voglio dei telefoni nella stanza, per favore"—"Prego."

5. L'ambulanza è persa, e il centro è vuoto.

☐ **Now cover up the answers below and translate the following:**

☐ *(You can write your answers in)*

1. Ciao, voglio dei polli.

2. La gamba sinistra e la gamba destra sono nel mare.

3. Grazie e buona notte. Sono molto stanco.

4. Mi scusi, ma voglio il telefono, per favore.

5. Piacere, sono molto brutto.

_____

_____

_____

_____

_____

_____

_____

_____

☐ *The answers are:*

1. Hello, I want some chickens.
2. The left leg and the right leg are in the sea.
3. Thank you and good night. I am very tired.
4. Excuse me, but I want the telephone, please.
5. How do you do, I am very ugly.

MONTHS

The months in Italian are quite similar in sound to the months in English, so no images will be given.

The Italian for *January* is *gennaio*

(pronounced JENN Y O—the Y is pronounced like the *y* in *my*)

ENGLISH	ITALIAN	PRONOUNCED
January	gennaio	JENN Y O
February	febbraio	FEBR Y O
March	marzo	MARTSO
April	aprile	APREELAY
May	maggio	MAJJO
June	giugno	JUNYO
July	luglio	LOOLYO
August	agosto	AGOSTO
September	settembre	SETTEMBRAY
October	ottobre	OTTOBRAY
November	novembre	NOVEMBRAY
December	dicembre	DEECHEMBRAY

☐ **Now cover up the answers below and translate the following:**

☐ *(You can write your answers in)*

1. In January, February, and March I drink the red wine.

2. In April, May, and June the sand is hot.

3. In July, August, and September the water is very dirty.

4. In October, November, and December the dogs are quiet.

5. In January, April, and September the bulls eat the flowers.

_____

_____

_____

_____

_____

_____

_____

☐ *The answers are:*

1. In gennaio, febbraio, e marzo bevo il vino rosso.

2. In aprile, maggio, e giugno la sabbia è calda.

3. In luglio, agosto, e settembre l'acqua è molto sporca.

4. In ottobre, novembre, e dicembre i cani sono tranquilli.

5. In gennaio, aprile, e settembre i tori mangiano i fiori.

This is the end of the course. We hope you have enjoyed it! Of course words and grammar will not be remembered forever without review, but if you look at the book from time to time, you will be surprised at how quickly everything comes back.

When you go abroad, do not be too shy to try out what you have learned. Your host will appreciate your making the effort to speak, even if you are sometimes wrong. And the more you attempt to speak, the more you will learn!

GLOSSARY

a	un, una, un'	butterfly	la farfalla
accident	l'incidente	button	il bottone
always	sempre	cabbage	il cavolo
am	sono	cake	la torta
ambulance	l'ambulanza	car	la macchina
and	e	carpet	il tappeto
apple	la mela	carrot	la carota
are (they)	sono	cashier	la cassa
at	a	castle	il castello
back	il dorso	cat	il gatto
bad	cattivo	caterpillar	il bruco
bandage	la fascia	chair	la sedia
bank	la banca	check	l'assegno
bathroom	il bagno	chicken	il pollo
battery	la batteria	church	la chiesa
bay	la baia	clean	pulito
bed	il letto	cloakroom	la guardaroba
bedroom	la camera	coffee	il caffè
bee	l'ape (fem.)	cold	freddo
bill	il conto	countryside	la campagna
bird	l'uccello	cow	la mucca
black	nero	cup	la tazza
blood	il sangue	cupboard	l'armadio
blouse	la blusa	currency	il cambio
blue	blu	exchange	
boat	il battello	curtain	la tenda
book	il libro	cushion	il cuscino
boss	il padrone	customs	la dogana
boy	il ragazzo	danger	il pericolo
brake	il freno	daughter	la figlia
bread	il pane	day	il giorno
breakdown	il guasto	dead	morto
bridge	il ponte	deep	profondo
brother	il fratello	dentist	il dentista
brown	marrone	dirty	sporco
bucket	la secchia	doctor	il dottore
bull	il toro	dog	il cane
but	ma	donkey	l'asino
butter	il burro	door	la porta

downtown	il centro	glass	il bicchiere
drawer	il cassetto	goat	la capra
dress	il vestito	golden	d'oro
drink (I)	bevo	good night	buona notte
drink (they)	bevono	goods	la merce
drinks (he/she)	beve	goose	l'oca
driver	l'autista	grass	l'erba
duck	l'anitra	gray	grigio
eat (I)	mangio	green	verde
eat (they)	mangiano	half	mezzo
eats (he/she)	mangia	hand	la mano
eggs	le uova	hard	duro
empty	vuoto	has (he/she)	ha
entrance	l'entrata	hat	il cappello
envelope	la busta	have (I)	ho
every	ogni	have (they)	hanno
excursion	la gita	head	la testa
exit	l'uscita	heart	il cuore
expensive	caro	heavy	pesante
factory	la fabbrica	hello	ciao
father	il padre	help	l'aiuto
fire	il fuoco	here	qui
firm	la ditta	high	alto
first	primo	hood	il cofano
fish	il pesce	horse	il cavallo
floor	il pavimento	hospital	l'ospedale
flower	il fiore	hot	caldo
fly	la mosca	hour	l'ora
foot	il piede	how do you do	piacere
fork	la forchetta	how much	quanto
fresh	fresco	husband	il marito
frog	la rana	in	in
from	da	insect	l'insetto
fruit	la frutta	is	è
full	pieno	it's a pleasure	prego
game	il gioco	jack	il cricco
garage	il garage	jacket	la giacca
garden	il giardino	jam	la marmellata
garlic	l'aglio	jellyfish	la medusa
gasoline	la benzina	kitchen	la cucina
girl	la ragazza	knife	il coltello

lake	il lago	oil	l'olio
lamb	l'agnello	omelette	la frittata
last	ultimo	on	su
lawyer	l'avvocato	onion	la cipolla
left	sinistro	only	solo
leg	la gamba	or	o
lemonade	la limonata	owner	il proprietario
less	meno	oyster	l'ostrica
letter	la lettera	pain	il dolore
lost	perso	passport	il passaporto
low	basso	path	il sentiero
manager	il direttore	pear	la pera
map	la mappa	pepper	il pepe
market	il mercato	piano	il pianoforte
meat	la carne	picnic	il picnic
melon	il melone	pig	il porco
menu	il menu	plant	la pianta
midday	il mezzogiorno	plate	il piatto
midnight	la mezzanotte	please	per favore
milk	il latte	police officer	il poliziotto
minute	il minuto	potato	la patata
mirror	lo specchio	price	il prezzo
mistake	l'errore	product	il prodotto
money	il denaro	put (I)	metto
month	il mese	put (they)	mettono
more	più	puts (he/she)	mette
morning	la mattina	quarter	quarto
mosquito	la zanzara	quick	rapido
mother	la madre	quiet	tranquillo
mountain	la montagna	rat	il topo
museum	il museo	red	rosso
mushroom	il fungo	restaurant	il ristorante
narrow	stretto	right	destro
newspaper	il giornale	river	il fiume
night	la notte	roof	il tetto
no	no	room	la stanza
noon	il mezzogiorno	rubber band	l'elastico
not	non	salary	il salario
now	adesso	salt	il sale
of	di	sand	la sabbia
office	l'ufficio	sea	il mare

second (adj)	secondo	thank you	grazie
second (noun)	il secondo	the	il, la, l', lo, i, gli, le
secretary	la segretaria		
see (I)	vedo	there	lì
see (they)	vedono	thief	il ladro
sees (he/she)	vede	thigh	la coscia
sell (I)	vendo	ticket	il biglietto
sell (they)	vendono	time	il tempo
sells (he/she)	vende	tire	la gomma
sheep	la pecora	tired	stanco
shirt	la camicia	to	a
shoe	la scarpa	toilet	il gabinetto
shop	il negozio	tomato	il pomodoro
sick	malato	tomorrow	domani
silver	argenteo	traffic lights	il semaforo
sister	la sorella	train	il treno
skin	la pelle	tree	l'albero
skirt	la gonna	trousers	i pantaloni
slow	lento	trout	la trota
small	piccolo	ugly	brutto
son	il figlio	vacation	le vacanze
soon	presto	veal	il vitello
sorry	mi scusi	very	molto
soup	la minestra	waiter	il cameriere
spark plug	la candela	want (I)	voglio
speak (I)	parlo	want (they)	vogliono
speak (they)	parlano	wants (he/she)	vuole
speaks (he/she)	parla	wasp	la vespa
spoon	il cucchiaio	water	l'acqua
staircase	la scala	week	la settimana
stamp	il francobollo	what	che
station	la stazione	wheel	la ruota
steak	la bistecca	where	dove
steering wheel	il volante	which	quale
stomach	lo stomaco	white	bianco
store clerk	la commessa	who	chi
street	la strada	why	perché
sun	il sole	wide	largo
table	la tavola	wife	la moglie
tea	il tè	window	la finestra
telephone	il telefono	wine	il vino

work	il lavoro		
worker	l'operaio		
year	l'anno		
yellow	giallo		
yes	sì		

Days of the Week

Sunday	domenica
Monday	lunedì
Tuesday	martedì
Wednesday	mercoledì
Thursday	giovedì
Friday	venerdì
Saturday	sabato

Months of the Year

January	gennaio
February	febbraio
March	marzo
April	aprile
May	maggio
June	giugno
July	luglio
August	agosto
September	settembre
October	ottobre
November	novembre
December	dicembre

Numbers

zero	zero
one	uno
two	due
three	tre
four	quattro
five	cinque
six	sei
seven	sette
eight	otto
nine	nove
ten	dieci
eleven	undici
twenty	venti
twenty-five	venticinque

FOREIGN LANGUAGE BOOKS AND MATERIALS

Spanish
Vox Spanish and English Dictionaries
Cervantes-Walls Spanish and English Dictionary
NTC's Dictionary of Spanish False Cognates
Complete Handbook of Spanish Verbs
Guide to Spanish Suffixes
Nice 'n Easy Spanish Grammar
Spanish Verbs and Essentials of Grammar
Spanish Verb Drills
Getting Started in Spanish
Guide to Spanish Idioms
Guide to Correspondence in Spanish
Diccionario Básico Norteamericano
Diccionario del Español Chicano
Basic Spanish Conversation
Let's Learn Spanish Picture Dictionary
My First Spanish and English Dictionary
Spanish Picture Dictionary
Welcome to Spain
Spanish for Beginners
Spanish à la Cartoon
El alfabeto
Let's Sing and Learn in Spanish
Let's Learn Spanish Coloring Book
Let's Learn Spanish Coloring Book-Audiocassette Package
My World in Spanish Coloring Book
Easy Spanish Word Games and Puzzles
Easy Spanish Crossword Puzzles
Easy Spanish Vocabulary Puzzles
Easy Spanish Word Power Games
How to Pronounce Spanish Correctly

French
NTC's New College French and English Dictionary
NTC's Dictionary of Faux Amis
NTC's Dictionary of Canadian French
French Verbs and Essentials of Grammar
Real French
Getting Started in French
Guide to French Idioms
Guide to Correspondence in French
Nice 'n Easy French Grammar
French à la Cartoon
French for Beginners
Let's Learn French Picture Dictionary
French Picture Dictionary
Welcome to France
The French-Speaking World
L'alphabet
Let's Learn French Coloring Book
Let's Learn French Coloring Book-Audiocassette Package
My World in French Coloring Book
French Verb Drills
Easy French Crossword Puzzles
Easy French Vocabulary Games
Easy French Grammar Puzzles
Easy French Word Games
Easy French Culture Games
How to Pronounce French Correctly
L'Express: Ainsi va la France
L'Express: Aujourd'hui la France
Le Nouvel Observateur: Arts, idées, spectacles
Au courant: Expressions for Communicating in
  Everyday French

Audio and Video Language Programs
Just Listen 'n Learn: Spanish, French, Italian,
  German, Greek, and Arabic
Just Listen 'n Learn PLUS: Spanish, French,
  and German
Conversational...in 7 Days: Spanish, French,
  German, Italian, Rusian, Greek, Portuguese
Practice & Improve Your...Spanish, French,
  German, and Italian
Practice & Improve Your...Spanish, French,
  German, and Italian PLUS
Improve Your...Spanish, French,
  German, and Italian: The P&I Method
VideoPassport French and Spanish

German
Schöffler-Weis German and English Dictionary
Klett German and English Dictionary
Das Max und Moritz Buch
NTC's Dictionary of German False Cognates
Getting Started in German
German Verbs and Essentials of Grammar
Guide to German Idioms
Street-wise German
Nice 'n Easy German Grammar
German à la Cartoon
Let's Learn German Picture Dictionary
German Picture Dictionary
German for Beginners
German Verb Drills
Easy German Crossword Puzzles
Easy German Word Games and Puzzles
Let's Learn German Coloring Book
Let's Learn German Coloring Book-Audiocassette Pack
My World in German Coloring Book
How to Pronounce German Correctly
Der Spiegel: Aktuelle Themen in der
  Bundesrepublik Deutschland

Italian
Zanichelli Super-Mini Italian and Dictionary
Zanichelli New College Italian and English Dictionary
Basic Italian Conversation
Getting Started in Italian
Italian Verbs and Essentials of Grammar
Let's Learn Italian Picture Dictionary
My World in Italian Coloring Book
Let's Learn Italian Coloring Book
Let's Learn Italian Coloring Book-Audiocassette Package
How to Pronounce Italian Correctly

Greek and Latin
NTC's New College Greek and English Dictionary
Essentials of Latin Grammar

Russian
Complete Handbook of Russian Verbs
Basic Structure Practice in Russian
Essentials of Russian Grammar
Business Russian
Roots of the Russian Language
Inspector General
Reading and Translating Contemporary Russian
How to Pronounce Russian

Polish
The Wiedza Powszechna Compact Polish and English
  Dictionary

Hebrew
Everyday Hebrew

Japanese
101 Japanese Idioms
Japanese in Plain English
Everyday Japanese
Japanese for Children
Japan Today!
Easy Hiragana
Easy Katakana
Easy Kana Workbook
How to Pronounce Japanese Correctly

Korean
Korean in Plain English

Chinese
Easy Chinese Phrasebook and Dictionary
Basic Chinese Vocabulary

Swedish
Swedish Verbs and Essentials of Grammar

Ticket to...Series
France, Germany, Spain, Italy (Guidebook and
  Audiocassette)

"Just Enough" Phrase Books
Chinese, Dutch, French, German, Greek, Hebrew,
  Hungarian, Italian, Japanese, Portuguese, Russian,
  Scandinavian, Serbo-Croat, Spanish
Business French, Business German, Business Spanish

PASSPORT BOOKS
a division of *NTC Publishing Group*
Lincolnwood, Illinois USA